For your children's
pleasure

Eileen Colwell

18. 7. 80

ALL THE YEAR ROUND

ALL THE YEAR ROUND

A COLLECTION OF SHORT STORIES AND POEMS TO BE READ ALOUD

SELECTED BY SHONA McKELLAR

EVANS BROTHERS LIMITED LONDON

First published 1980 by Evans Brothers Limited.
Montague House, Russell Square, London WC1B 5BX

This selection © 1980 Evans Brothers Limited
The copyright of each story remains the property
of the author.

British Library Cataloguing in Publication Data

All the year round.
  1. Children's literature, English
  I. McKellar, Shona
  820'.8'09282   PZ5
  ISBN 0–237–45513–7

For permission to reproduce copyright material the Editor and
Publishers are indebted to the authors and the following:

Doubleday & Co Inc for "The Green Spring" by Shan Mei from
Twentieth Century Chinese Poetry, © 1963 Kai-uy Hsu; Anne
English for "Traffic Jam" and "Dark Windy Night"; The Friends
of the Girls' Public Day School Trust c/o Peterborough Literary
Agency for "Janik and the Magic Balls" and "Joseph and the
Trees" by Rhoda Power; Gerda Mayer for "January Moon";
Outpost Publications for "The May Tree" by Norah Hussey from
Brooks and Blossoms; Oxford University Press for "Fireworks" by
James Reeves from *The Blackbird in the Lilac*; Caroline Freeman
Sayer for "Spring Wind"; The Society of Authors and Miss
Pamela Hinkson for "August Weather" by Katharine Tynan.

Photoset by Northampton Phototypesetters Ltd
Printed and bound in Great Britain by
William Clowes (Beccles) Limited, Beccles and London
PRA 6832

Contents

The Garden Year

January brings the snow,
Makes our feet and fingers glow.

February brings the rain,
Thaws the frozen lake again.

March brings breezes, loud and shrill,
To stir the dancing daffodil.

April brings the primrose sweet,
Scatters daisies at our feet.

May brings flocks of pretty lambs,
Skipping by their fleecy dams.

June brings tulips, lilies, roses,
Fills the children's hands with posies.

Hot July brings cooling showers,
Apricots and gillyflowers.

August brings the sheaves of corn,
Then the harvest home is borne.

Warm September brings the fruit;
Sportsmen then begin to shoot.

Fresh October brings the pheasant;
Then to gather nuts is pleasant.

Dull November brings the blast;
Then the leaves are whirling fast.

Chill December brings the sleet,
Blazing fire, and Christmas treat.

Sara Coleridge

The Crevice by the River Bank

Donald Bisset

Once upon a time there was a little crack in the earth which was part of a river bank. The crack was about a centimetre wide and half a metre deep. It was called a crevice.

It was rather a thoughtful crevice. Some ants lived in it. They liked it there, especially on cold January days. There was no wind down there and though it was rather dark the ants didn't mind.

But the crevice had a little pain. In fact it had four little pains. They didn't hurt much but the crevice couldn't think why they were there.

Then it remembered it had felt a similar pain the year before. But it had had only one pain then. It was like having a tiny lump inside. It even felt nice in a way, but strange.

The river gurgled gently by, on its·way through the countryside. The river and the crevice were great friends.

"I've got four little pains!" said the crevice to the river.

"Good!" said the river.

"Good?"

"Think," said the river. "Try and remember the story of what happened before."

"I will," said the crevice, and this is the story.

The crevice had felt a pain and then it had felt a tickle. The ants were asleep. It wasn't them being tickly.

What was it?

"I've got a tickle," said the crevice to the river.

"One tickle?" asked the river.

"Yes."

"I've got a hundred and forty-six tickles," said the river.

"Is it the swans and the cygnets swishing their legs through you that makes you tickly?"

"No! The swans aren't tickly. They feel rather nice."

"Is it the Kingfisher skimming your water with its wings?"

"No. You see," said the river, "it's spring-time now and a hundred and forty-six water fleas have just been born. They are tickly water fleas."

"But why have *I* got a tickle?" said the crevice.

"The ants, perhaps!" said the river.

"No, they're asleep."

"Perhaps it's something different. Something growing inside you."

"Oh!" The crevice *was* excited. "I wonder what it is? Let me think. Spring-time on a river bank. It could be: Water violet, Meadow grass, Ragged Robin."

"I don't think it's any of those," said the river. "Look, down there, there's a coot building its nest."

"But what about my tickle?" said the crevice.

"Wait and see," said the river. "I think I know what it is."

"Is it going to be nice?"

"Very, very nice!"

The crevice waited.

A long green stalk grew inside it.

"What are you stalk?" said the crevice. "Are you a flower stalk? Are you going to be a flower?"

It *was* going to be a flower. But it was asleep. It hadn't been born properly, yet.

So the crevice waited, and waited, and waited.

The swallows came and began to fly about. The mother coot laid some eggs. The boy mallards said to the girl mallards that they liked girl mallards better than anything in the world.

Still the crevice waited.   .

Spring passed by, the oak and the ash and the maple tree buds all burst into leaf. Foxes came out of the place where they lived and looked for food to take back to the baby foxes that had just been born. Wood pigeons cooed in the woods.

"I think it must be summer-time," thought the crevice.

Hundreds of buttercups were growing nearby.

"I wish I had a buttercup growing in me!" thought the crevice. It looked up at the bud at the end of the long stalk coming from deep inside it. As it watched the bud began to open a tiny bit.

The crevice watched it every day and one morning as the sun was shining it opened right out.

"I've got a buttercup, after all!" thought the crevice. But the buttercup grew and grew till it was bigger than all the other buttercups.

"That's a kingcup!" said the river.

9

The summer passed. The baby coots and cygnets grew up and the weather began to get colder. The beautiful kingcup which closed its petals every night and opened them as soon as it was light began to droop a little and then its petals began to curl up and drop off.

"Have you got any seeds inside you?" said the crevice.

"Yes, I have!" said the kingcup. "And that dragonfly on the water-lily perched on me lots of times and I think my seeds are going to be proper seeds and will grow baby kingcups. The wind will blow them away and they will fall on the ground and next year they will become kingcups, too."

The weather became colder still and the swallows were perched on twigs and railings and telegraph wires, waiting to fly away to warm places in the south of the world.

Now, it grew colder and the swans flew away with their children who had learned to fly. But other swans had arrived who didn't mind the cold. "We are whooper swans!" they said to the mallard ducks who had stayed, along with the kingfisher. The wind blew all the leaves off the trees. They looked bare and beautiful against the grey sky.

The crevice was still remembering.

"What happened after that?" said the river. "Can you remember?"

"That was in December," thought the crevice. "It was nearly Christmas."

"Do you remember it was very cold and you wanted a blanket to keep your seed warm," said the river.

"Did I? I didn't know I had a seed."

"There were seeds in the earth all along my banks," said the river. "I think you knew in a sort of way."

"I think I did!" said the crevice. "Then what happened on Christmas morning?"

"The snow fell."

"So it did!" said the crevice. "The snowflakes flew down softly, thousands of them, and made a lovely warm blanket of snow."

"That was your Christmas present!" said the river. "Then when January came you felt a tiny pain."

"Four pains!" said the crevice. "And that's now, this January!"

"Yes!"

"Have I got four seeds inside me?"
"Yes."
"Buttercup seeds?"
"Kingcup seeds," said the river.
"Four kingcup seeds!" said the crevice. "Then I'll have four stalks and, in the spring, four little buds and in the summer, four beautiful kingcups."
The river rippled by.
The days grew longer.
A swallow appeared.
The crevice was very, very happy.

January Moon

The moon skates through the sky
Against the wind, against
The low-flying clouds.
On blue ice she dances
Soundlessly.

Gerda Mayer

Good-bye Old House

Jeremy Strong

John did not want to move. Nor for that matter did his cat, Snuff. The two of them sat on a large cardboard box in the hall and watched. It seemed as if the whole house was being packed up in boxes – big boxes, small boxes, all full of different things.

Mum and Dad were rushing about shouting at each other. Everything was being moved, from the largest wardrobe to the smallest pair of socks. Nothing was going to be left behind.

An enormous lorry arrived and two cheerful men and a cross-patch driver came to help. They began loading all the boxes and cupboards, plants and chairs, into the back of the lorry.

Snuff jumped off the box and slid under a chair to hide from the noise and confusion. Her tail twitched from side to side nervously. John wondered what was going to happen to Snuff.

"She's coming with us, of course," said Dad. "We shan't leave her behind. Come on Snuff." But Snuff didn't want to come. Dad had to chase her in and out of all the rooms in the house, with Snuff dodging this way and that.

Then the cat saw the ladder going up into the loft. Snuff paused at the bottom of the ladder with one paw on the first rung. She looked up at the dark hiding hole.

"No Snuff!" cried Dad. "Don't go up there! SNUFF!!" It was too late. The cat was scared by Dad's yelling and she shot up the ladder and into the loft. Dad climbed wearily after her.

He switched on the attic light. There was Snuff, looking at Dad, very coldly, from among the water pipes.

"Come on Snuff," coaxed Dad, as he moved closer. Snuff jumped up on to the cold water tank.

"Come here. I'll give you two plates of fish tonight." Snuff turned and jumped down from the tank. She slunk away into the corner.

Then Dad tripped over the water pipes, he put out his arm to save himself from falling and plunged it straight into the cold water tank. His sleeve was soaked.

"Have you caught her yet?" asked John from down in the hall.

12

"Almost," shouted Dad hopefully, shaking the water off his hand.

Dad was up in the attic for another twenty minutes. He cut his forehead on a low rafter, grazed his other arm, and tore one of his trouser legs on a rusty nail. Then Snuff tried to dodge between his legs and Dad managed to grab her by the tail and scoop her up.

At last the lorry men came and said that they were ready to go.

"We got everything in," said the cross-patch driver, "though I don't know how we managed. Practically broke my back carrying that big mirror of yours."

It was time to leave. Dad put Snuff in the back of the car with John. "Well," he said, "it's good-bye old house, hello new house." John looked out of the car window as Dad drove off. He felt sad.

On the way to the new house Snuff made a mess on the car floor. Dad stopped and Mum cleaned it up.

"She's never done anything like that before," said John anxiously.

"She must be ill."

"I expect she's frightened," said Dad. "She doesn't want to leave."

"Neither do I," said John. "Can't we take everything back to the old place? She'll be all right then, won't she?"

"We can't go back now," said Mum. "We've got a new place to go to."

John had only seen the new house once. When the car pulled up outside, it was just as he had remembered it – cold and empty.

But Mum and Dad seemed very enthusiastic as they walked around the rooms with their endless blank walls and bare floors. They kept saying how smashing it was, and look at the rooms, and how much bigger the kitchen was.

"I like small kitchens," John said.

"You wouldn't if you had to work in them," smiled Mum.

Snuff was shut in the new big kitchen. "We don't want her to escape," Dad said.

"Why should she want to escape?" asked John.

"She's probably upset by the move. Cats don't like moving. It takes them a little while to settle down." John could hear Snuff scratching on the other side of the kitchen door, trying to get out.

"Come and see your new bedroom," Dad suggested. They all trooped upstairs. John's bedroom was quite empty.

"Isn't it smashing?" said Mum, but the bedroom seemed so cold to John. Bare walls, bare floor, and not even a lampshade. It was like a big empty box with a window at one end.

"It's horrible," said John. Before Mum and Dad could say anything they were interrupted by a lot of noise from downstairs.

The lorry had arrived and everything was being unloaded and unpacked. It took a very long time. John was in bed and asleep before they had finished. He had to sleep on the hard camp-bed in the sitting room downstairs because none of his things had been unpacked yet.

When he woke up in the morning John went straight to the kitchen to see Snuff, but she wasn't there. John immediately searched the other rooms, looking among the half-filled packing cases, but there was no sign of Snuff.

Dad looked for her, and so did Mum, but they could not find her. John felt as if he was going to cry, but he didn't.

"Don't worry," said Mum. "She's probably gone back to the old house because she likes it there."

"I like it there," sniffed John. "I want to go back too."

"We'll go back now," said Dad.

"For ever?"

"Let's just go and see if Snuff is waiting for us."

When they got to the old house John ran straight into the garden calling for Snuff, but there was no sign of her. Dad shouted even louder.

After a few minutes there was a rustling in the hedge and Snuff appeared and ran straight to John, who clutched her with both arms.

"There," said Dad happily. "I thought she'd be here. Now let's go and look at the old house."

When they got inside John found that the place was quite empty. It was like a shell. There was nothing in it at all to show that he had ever lived there. They went upstairs and peered into John's old bedroom. It was like a large empty box with a window at one end, bare and cold, without even a lampshade.

John frowned and he picked up Snuff and carried her back to the car. On the return journey Snuff sat quietly on John's lap. As soon as Snuff went into the new house she wandered from room to room sniffing at all the things she recognized. John wandered through the house too, noticing where things had been put.

By the evening John's new bedroom looked just like his old one with his own bedspread on his old bed. There was his toy box, his books, his old chest of drawers. Even his pictures were up on the walls. Snuff came and curled up at the end of his bed.

John felt a bit easier. He went over to the window and looked out. There were several trees in the new garden. They looked as if he could spend a lot of time climbing them. There were more trees here than there were at the old house. John lay back in his own bed and closed his eyes. Perhaps it wasn't going to be so bad here after all, he thought.

Jeremy Jumbletop

Anne Lidall

Jeremy Jumbletop was a very strange man. He did everything the wrong way round.

He walked backwards. He sat backwards on his chair.

When he went to bed he put on all his clothes, including his hat and his boots, and when he got up he put on his pyjamas and went to work.

He slept in the day-time and worked at night.

All his life people had tried to make Jeremy Jumbletop do things the proper way.

"You're very silly, Jeremy Jumbletop," they used to say. "Whoever heard of anyone starting his dinner with pudding and finishing with soup? It's nonsense, and you ought to change your ways."

But Jeremy Jumbletop didn't care. He liked to do things the wrong way round. He was very happy. Even when he read the newspaper upside down it made perfect sense to him, and although he stood on his head to watch television he enjoyed it just as much as anyone else.

The strange thing was that some of his ways were very useful to other people. Because he was so good at skating backwards he was able to teach people to skate forwards. And he was quite a champion at tug-of-war, because pulling backwards came so naturally to him.

He went on holiday in the winter-time, of course, riding in the train, with his back to the engine, and arriving at the seaside in the middle of the night. He stayed in a caravan which he had turned upside down because he liked it better that way, although he had to admit that he did keep falling out of his bunk when he had just nodded off to sleep.

One night when he was on holiday at the seaside he decided to go for a walk. He was walking backwards along the beach when he thought he heard a cry for help. He was a little surprised at first, because it was two o'clock in the morning, very, very dark, and bitterly cold, and all the people who did things the proper way round were tucked up in bed.

16

He listened again. Yes, there was certainly somebody calling.

"Who's there?" he shouted above the noise of the wind and the rain.

"Help me!" said a voice.

"Where are you?" asked Jeremy Jumbletop.

"Here I am," answered the voice. "Up here, on the cliff. I'm stuck on a ledge and it's so dark that I dare not move an inch for fear of falling down."

"I'll come and get you," said Jeremy Jumbletop.

"No, no!" cried the voice. "You couldn't possibly find me. Go along to the coastguard's house and get him to bring some lights and a good strong rope. That's the only way I can be saved."

"Oh, very well," said Jeremy Jumbletop. "I'll do as you say, but I'm afraid the coastguard will be very cross when I wake him up."

He ran backwards along the beach until he came to the coastguard's house. As he had feared, the coastguard was not at all pleased to be woken up in the middle of such a dreadful night.

"How did you come to be on the beach at this time of night?" he said.

"I was taking a walk," said Jeremy Jumbletop.

"What a silly thing to do," said the coastguard. "I never heard of such a thing. Are you quite sure there is a man trapped on a ledge?"

"Oh yes," said Jeremy Jumbletop.

The coastguard reluctantly roused several of his friends and they all set off together along the top of the cliff until they came to the place where the man was trapped. "He's down there," said Jeremy Jumbletop.

Sure enough, they heard the trapped man crying out. Lights were brought to the scene and the men peered over the edge of the cliff.

"Can you wait until daylight?" they cried.

"No, no, I shall freeze to death," came the reply. "Do hurry."

The men shook their heads.

"We can't go down there," they said. "Even with ropes we shall have to lead him backwards along the ledge and who is going to do that? We need someone who has eyes in the back of his head!"

And they all looked at Jeremy Jumbletop.

"You can walk backwards," they said. "And you can climb downwards without looking where you are going."

"Of course I can," said Jeremy Jumbletop. "I told the man I would help him but he wouldn't believe me.

Jeremy Jumbletop tied a rope around his waist and went backwards down the cliff quite easily. He took hold of the man's hands and led him along the ledge to safety.

Everybody said how brave Jeremy Jumbletop had been, but he only shook his head.

"It was quite easy," he said.

All the same, the people in the seaside town made a great fuss of him. They gave him a dinner at seven o'clock in the morning, and he had upside-down cake and sausages with the skins inside. Then he put on his very best suit and went to bed.

Jeremy Jumbletop was no doubt a very strange man. He went on doing things the wrong way round for the rest of his life, but nobody made fun of him any more, because he had proved how very useful he could be.

The queen gave him a medal, and can you guess where he wore it?

That's right. On his back.

Ponkyfoot

David Parker

There was once a terrible pirate called Ponkyfoot. Ponkyfoot was the most dangerous pirate who ever was, and whenever another pirate heard his name his face would turn as white as his toe-nails and his hands would flutter in the breeze. Ponkyfoot was called Ponky for short.

From a distance Ponky looked a bit like a barrel of tar with a red scarf wound around the top. Just below the scarf, his black eyebrows twitched like crabs' nippers and his black eyes bulged like cannon-balls and his angry face was as red as boiling tomatoes.

But the very worst thing about Ponkyfoot was his left leg which was short and thick. It was made from an old ship's timber and it ended in a peg. So that wherever Ponkyfoot walked the leg made a noise so horrible, it would turn your blood to seawater. Ponk! Ponk! Ponk! it went, and everyone else's feet would shake in their boots like jellyfish.

In the harbour below the town lay Ponkyfoot's ship, the bad ship *Thunderbone*. Her hull was as black as her pirate captain, and her decks were red, like his angry face.

One night when there was no moon, and the stars were covered with clouds and the water was dark and cold as death, Ponkyfoot decided to put to sea.

"I'll hunt a fine ship and blow her to pieces and leave her sailors in the sea," he thought, "or if there aren't any fine ships to fire at I'll battle with one of me pirate enemies and sink *his* bones to the bottom," and he smiled a horrible smile.

Ponkyfoot looked down fiercely on his scowling pirate crew, standing before him on the fiery deck of *Thunderbone*. There stood Ironhead, his huge hand on a cutlass with a blade as wide as a plank. A scar ran from his nose to his ear and his bald head shone like oil. At the wheel was the grim pirate known as Oyster, saying nothing. He opened his mouth only to eat. Not far from him was a strange figure with a gag in his mouth, jumping up and down. His name was Manywords and he was greatly feared by the other men because he drove them mad with endless talk that no one could understand. Behind the group of frightful men on the deck was perhaps the worst of them all, the great round shape of the evil pirate cook, Glob. These, and the rest of Ponkyfoot's angry crew, stood waiting for their captain's order to sail, as the cold wind cut into their cruel faces.

Ponkyfoot looked over the side, down into the black water flowing past his ship. The tide was beginning to turn. He lifted his head and shouted a command and the strong wind carried his voice like a scrap of paper. The pirates ran over the deck at once. Some of them laid hold of the capstan and others climbed the rigging. Oyster stood ready at the wheel and Glob disappeared below like a squid sliding into a hole. As they worked at their evil ship they sang a terrible song:

> Thunder and smoke and blood and bone –
> Away, boys, together!
> Fear no dead men, cold as stone –
> Never, boys, never!

Slowly, the sails filled, and the anchor came dripping out of the sea. Oyster spun the great wheel and *Thunderbone* moved silently out of the harbour and began to rise and fall to the long sea swell. Soon there was no sound on deck but the creaking of spars and ropes and the crash of the sea as the pirate ship lifted and plunged her head like a salty horse. Oyster stood silent as stone at the wheel, gripping its wooden spokes with his thick fingers and looking out into the darkness.

Ponkyfoot paced the deck. Now and then he would clamp his long brass telescope to his eye, looking for signs of a ship he could chase and fight and plunder. But he could see nothing except the grey sea and the white, broken waves. He became angry.

"It's time I found a ship," he growled. "I want gold and dead men's bones." Ponky turned to face his crew. "We want gold, and dead men's bones, don't we lads?" he roared. A fierce shout rose from the men on the deck. Ironhead began to call out a chorus in the howling wind and every pirate on deck lifted his head and joined in the terrible song.

> Bones of ships and bones of men shining in the sun,
> Aye! Give us blood and give us gold and give us Spanish rum!

At that moment, Ponkyfoot heard the sound of a great bell. He saw every one of his pirate crew go stiff with fright. At once the sea was covered with fog. The wind dropped, until there was only the noise of the rocking ship. Then the sound of the bell came again. Every sailor peered out into the fog. Ponkyfoot swung his telescope from one side to another, but he could see nothing, only the swirling mist and the water lying at the sides of the ship. The bell sounded again with a great clang.

"It's the ghost ship," they began to mutter to one another, "the ship no sailor has ever seen and lived to speak of." Whoever saw the ghost ship would join her crew, old sailormen used to say.

Ponky's heart started to bang, his sword shook in his belt and his pipe went out at once. His hands gripped the rails of his ship and his eyes turned towards the place in the fog from which the sound had come. Still he could see nothing. Once again the bell sounded across the water and Ponkyfoot and his pirate crew saw through the cold mist the form of a ship moving silently towards them.

Ponky and his pirates stood quite still on the deck of *Thunderbone*, staring in fear as the ghost ship came nearer. In perfect silence it came closer until it drew alongside *Thunderbone*. At last Ponkyfoot saw its crew.

"They're skeletons!" Ponky whispered. "The bones of dead sailormen!"

White and stiff the sailors of the ghost ship stood upon the deck, and a skeleton held the wheel. Within a moment, the terrible ship sailed by, the mist closed around her, and she was gone.

At that very moment a bell sounded with a loud, "Bong!" Ponkyfoot opened his mouth wide to shout in fear but no sound would come. He gripped the ship's rail and stared out at the grey water. He saw only a great bell rolling in the sea-mist, nodding its head like a sleepy old man. A sea-bird rode on its top, rolling from side to side in the green waves.

"We've seen enough, lads!" Ponky shouted to his pirate crew. "We've seen the ghost ship, that carries off dead sailormen. We'll chase and fight no more. We'll go about and drive for home lads! Let her run before the wind, away from mist and bones and the ghost ship come to take us."

Soon the shining black ship turned, and began to cut through the sharp, cold waves. Her sails banged and stretched, and *Thunderbone* ran hard towards the sun at the edge of the sea.

But Ponkyfoot and his pirate crew and the bad ship *Thunderbone* were never seen again – not at sea, and not in the harbour. Some people say Ponky has sailed to an island no one has ever seen. But old sailormen talk instead of the ghost ship that carries off dead men. When the sea is wild and the wind is loud and running through the town, *then* you'll hear old Ponky's ghost, they say. When the night is black and full of storm you'll hear his wooden leg. Ponk! Ponk! Ponk! it goes, ringing through the streets. And doors and windows slam and bang and the town goes straight to bed.

Snowdrops

I like to think
  That, long ago,
There fell to earth
  Some flakes of snow
Which loved this cold,
  Grey world of ours
So much, they stayed
  As snowdrop flowers.

Mary Vivian

The Pancake

Mix a pancake,
Stir a pancake,
Pop it in the pan.

Fry the pancake,
Toss the pancake,
Catch it if you can.

Christina Rossetti

Mrs Lurkin's Pancakes

Muriel Pearson

The first pancake Mrs Lurkin made was so heavy that it slid off the pan and flopped to the floor with a thud. It was round and thick, and Mrs Lurkin gasped with dismay as the pancake rolled slowly out of the door and into the street. It gathered speed and soon disappeared out of sight.

"That *was* a calamity!" said Mrs Lurkin. "But I shall try again." Before getting her mixing bowl ready, she shut the door tightly. But each pancake she made was just as round and heavy as the first one. Nobody could eat pancakes like that.

"This really is a calamity," sighed Mrs Lurkin as she heard a knock at the door. It was Mr Smith delivering groceries from his shop.

"Good morning," said Mr Smith as he brought his box into the kitchen. "Why, what lovely wheels you've made! I could do with four of those for my van."

Mrs Lurkin happily gave Mr Smith four round heavy pancakes. She watched him drive away in his van with the new pancake wheels.

"Good morning, Mrs Lurkin." This time it was the cobbler. "I've mended your shoes."

The cobbler brought the shoes into the kitchen.

"I see you've been making tops for three-legged stools," he remarked. "I should like one for my shop please."

Mrs Lurkin happily gave the cobbler a new top for his three-legged stool. She watched him walk along the street, with the round heavy pancake tucked under his arm.

Just then the postman appeared, wheeling his bicycle. He was not in a very good temper.

"Good morning, Mrs Lurkin," said the postman. "I have just been knocked off my bicycle by a heavy rolling pancake. Wait till I catch the person who made it."

"Oh, what a calamity," sighed Mrs Lurkin. She took another book from her shelf to find a different recipe for pancakes. And she made another mixture in her mixing bowl.

This time she was able to toss the pancakes easily, as they were so light, and she watched in surprise as the pancakes floated out of the window. They floated high up into the sky and looked like little cream-coloured clouds. They were very pretty, but nobody can eat pancakes which float into the sky.

"Another calamity," sighed Mrs Lurkin as she tried another time. Again the pancakes were so light that they floated out into the garden, landing on a prickly bush, where they looked like enormous flowers.

"This is indeed a day of calamities," sighed Mrs Lurkin, though she was quite proud to have the only pancake bush in town. But she wanted to be able to *eat* her pancakes.

So Mrs Lurkin set off to the library and chose five books with pancake recipes.

Over the weekend she read them very carefully.

On Monday, she got up early, determined to make the best pancakes in town. She used the recipe from the first book.

"Oh, what a calamity!" gasped Mrs Lurkin as every pancake she made turned out to be square!

So she took them all out to her little, green, garden shed and stacked them on the shelves.

On Tuesday, she used the recipe in the second book. She was not at all pleased to see that each pancake had a round hole right in the middle.

"Oh dear, another calamity," she said, as she piled the pancakes on to plates and took them out to the green, garden shed.

On Wednesday, she bravely tried a third recipe. This time her pancakes were shaped like tennis balls and bounced out of the pan.

"This is indeed a week of calamities," moaned Mrs Lurkin. She gathered the balls into a large basket and took them out to the green, garden shed.

On Thursday, Mrs Lurkin's pancakes were shaped like animals and birds.

There were dog-shaped pancakes, cat-shaped pancakes and chicken-shaped pancakes. There was even an elephant-shaped pancake with a long trunk and a little tail.

"It's just one calamity after another," sighed Mrs Lurkin, as she piled all the animal-shaped pancakes on to a tray and carried them to the green, garden shed. By this time the shelves were almost full with pancakes of all shapes and sizes.

On Friday, Mrs Lurkin tried the recipe in the fifth and last book.

To her dismay she found that the pancake mixture was turning into letters of the alphabet.

"Another calamity," she said, as she hung the letters of the alphabet on a line in the garden shed.

"At least they all smell good," remarked Mrs Lurkin. "But why can't I make plain ordinary pancakes?"

And she gathered up the five books and returned them to the library.

Next morning Mrs Lurkin woke up to hear strange noises. They were coming from the street. She looked out of her bedroom window and was very surprised to see a long, long line of people queueing in the street.

"I wonder why all those people are waiting there," she murmured to herself as she got dressed.

She was just about to put on the kettle when there was a knock at the door.

"Good morning Mrs Lurkin," said the lady at the door. "When are you opening your pancake shop?"

"My pancake shop?" asked Mrs Lurkin, her eyes growing big with surprise. All the people had smelt the lovely pancake smell which was coming from the green garden shed and now they were queueing to buy Mrs Lurkin's pancakes.

Soon she was supplying everybody with her strange pancakes. Some people wanted the square pancakes as they would fit nicely into their sandwich boxes while the children liked the animal-shaped pancakes and the ones that bounced. But it was the teachers who chose the pancakes shaped like letters of the alphabet.

"This is not a calamity after all," said Mrs Lurkin cheerfully, and in no time at all she had sold every single pancake. She closed the door of the green, garden shed and set off to the library. She wanted to borrow the five books again. Mrs Lurkin was going to be very, very busy next week, getting ready for Pancake Day.

Blanco the White Mouse

June Glover

One cold night Henry fieldmouse heard a tap at the door and looked out. At first he could see nothing but swirling snowflakes. Then, out of the snow came a strange sight, it was a mouse just like Henry but white all over from ears to tail.

"A snowmouse!" exclaimed Henry.

"Not at all," replied the other, rather proudly. "I'm a white mouse. My name is Blanco. I'm very cold, may I come in?"

Henry invited the white mouse in and shared his tiny supper with him. Then they snuggled down to sleep.

In the morning Blanco told Henry he lived in a house with two boys, called Barney and Bobby. He had a warm cage, plenty to eat and toys to play with.

"But I got bored. Everything was done for me. I wanted some excitement," he said. "So I ran away. I think I'll live in the woods with you."

Henry explained that food was very difficult to find in the woods in winter. They would have to go out and hunt for something for breakfast.

Henry and Blanco returned from their hunt very cold and still rather hungry.

"I don't like it here after all," complained Blanco. "I wish I'd stayed in my cage now."

"You'll soon grow to love it in the woods," said Henry.

But he was wrong.

Blanco wouldn't go out because it was too cold. And, when he stayed in, he said Henry's home was too small and uncomfortable.

"Oh I'm so hungry," he would groan. But, when Henry brought him food, he said, "I don't like it, it tastes nasty."

Henry was rather tired of having to look after Blanco but he told himself it would be better when spring came. He was wrong.

"I can't go out now the snow's gone," moaned Blanco. "My white fur would show up against the brown earth and I'd be caught by wild beasts and eaten."

Henry sighed. It was no good, he would have to take Blanco back home somehow. But where was his home?

He decided to try Farmer Brown's house first, as it was the nearest to the woods.

It was still a long way for mice to travel and it took a whole day. Blanco, as usual, grumbled all the time.

The most dangerous part of the journey was crossing the farmyard, which was inhabited by fierce dogs and cats.

"I can't possibly run across there!" shivered Blanco. "I'm much too frightened."

"Come on," Henry urged him. "You're nearly home now."

But when they were inside the house Blanco decided that it wasn't his home after all. Henry's heart sank. Would he have to take Blanco all the way back to the woods?

Suddenly the white mouse changed his mind. "Yes – I can see my cage up there!" he squeaked.

He ran up on to the table and into the cage, slamming the door shut behind him.

Poor Henry was left alone on the table. He froze with terror as two noisy humans burst into the room. It was Barney and Bobby, who shouted with pleasure to see Blanco.

Then, "Hello, there's a fieldmouse," said Barney. "Perhaps he's brought Blanco home."

"Better take him back to the woods," said Bobby.

He took Henry gently in his hands and carried him across the farmyard, putting him down safely on the woodland path.

"Thank you for looking after Blanco," he whispered.

The Green Spring

When spring comes
I see the woods turning green,
The water in the river turning green,
The hills turning green,
The fields turning green,
The little beetles turning green,
And even the white-bearded old man turning green.
The green blood
Nurtures the fatigued earth,
And from the earth bursts forth
A green hope.

Shan Mei

Spring Wind

Swishing in the branches,
Rattling the doors,
Whistling over chimneys,
Moaning under floors.
Tugging at the birds' wings,
Maddening the cats,
Jangling the aerials,
Chasing all the hats.
In and out of everywhere,
On and on it goes –
Dogs and children love it
When the spring wind blows.

Caroline Freeman Sayer

The Two Robins

Ruth Ainsworth

There were once two robins who were ready to build a nest and lay their eggs. They knew exactly how to make it, but they could not find a suitable place.

First they tried the barn. The swallows were flying in and out, making their cup-shaped nests on the rafters. When they saw the robins they said, "There's no room for any more nests. We have too many of our own. Go away!"

So the robins flew sadly away.

The next place they found was a little wooden house, with an open door and straw on the floor. The straw will be very useful, they thought, and they set to work.

Then Rip, the farm dog, came into the little house. "This is my kennel," he barked. "I can't have birds flying in and out at all hours. And then baby birds squeaking and squawking and always wanting to be fed. Go away!"

So the robins flew sadly away.

Nearby was a much larger wooden house with straw on the floor. It was quiet and dark and did not look like a kennel. Surely there's plenty of room for us here, thought the robins. They saw some feathers among the straw and they felt that it was a welcome sight. So they set to work.

Then a large, angry hen, with her feathers fluffed out and her comb bright red, came clucking through the door.

"This is a hen-house," she cackled. "Twelve hens sleep here at night. We can't possibly have robins as well. You might peck our eggs or steal our corn. Go away, do!"

So the robins flew sadly away. They didn't even wait to explain that they *never* pecked eggs, and would not dream of stealing corn.

"Let's try somewhere a bit higher," said Father Robin. "What about those elm trees? I believe there are some untidy nests at the top already. We'll build lower down, nearer the ground, out of the way."

So they set to work and got on quite well. They had nearly finished the outside of the nest when the rooks, who lived at the top of the trees, came home in a great, black, cawing crowd. They flapped their wings in the robins' faces and said rudely, "These are our trees. Rooks always live together, and these elms belong to us. We can't have any other birds living so near. Go away!"

So the robins flew sadly away.

The next day they hadn't the heart to go far, looking for a good place. They happened to visit the stable which smelt warm and comfortable. An old ragged coat hung on a nail. Mother Robin peeped into one of its pockets which already contained a piece of string, some used matches and some hair.

"This is the very place," she said. "And these odds and ends will help with the nest."

When the nest was finished, and the eggs laid, and Mother Robin was keeping them warm, the farmer remembered his old coat. He went to the stable, put it on and slipped his hand into his pocket. He felt warm, feathered Mother Robin, trembling with fear. Father Robin was flying up and down anxiously.

The farmer guessed at once what had happened.

"Well, I never! If a robin hasn't made a nest in the pocket of my old coat," he exclaimed, taking it off very gently and hanging it back on the nail. "I've done without this coat for several weeks and never missed it. I can do without it for a bit longer. Don't you be fussed, my pretties. You'll come to no harm, that I'll promise."

The eggs hatched and the babies grew feathers and learned to fly. It was a proud day when they flew off, leaving their father and mother to have a little rest.

The young robins looked such fine youngsters that even the swallows, and Rip the dog, and the hens, and the rooks, admired them.

"How lucky we were to find such a good place for the nest," said Father Robin."

"And such a very, very kind farmer," said Mother Robin.

What Happened on Bunch Hill

Mary Sullivan

At the bottom of Bunch Hill there's an absolutely smashing play-ground. Instead of ordinary swings there are boat-shaped ones, the kind they have at fairs, with seats at each end and ropes to work them hanging down in the middle. They go amazingly high, and come down in a rush just when you think they're going to turn right over.

In another corner there's a rocking horse which isn't a horse at all; it's a dragon with six seats on his back, and red-iron breath coming out of his mouth.

There's also a roundabout shaped like a flying-saucer, with smooth silver sides, and things like antennae to hold on by.

The climbing-frame is made of logs, with a tree-house at the top, and a rope-ladder at the back for quick getaways.

There are other things to play on, too, and there's a real snow-white goat in a pen. His name is Banjo, and he chews your clothes whenever he can get at them.

At the top of Bunch Hill there's a flat grassy place with no trees around. From there you can see all over the town. People fly kites up there, especially on Sundays.

It was March, and a bit more blowy, and so Dad started talking about flying the kite again. He says he made it for Jerry and me, but whenever we fly it from Bunch Hill, Dad says, "Patrick! Hold this end!" and "Put your finger on this knot, Jerry!" and "Hang on to this and don't move!" all the morning long. We hold the string, and put our fingers on the knots, and enviously stare down at the children swooping in the swing-boats and skimming on the flying-saucer.

Dad's kite is nearly as tall as he is. It is blue and yellow, and has a great many struts and fins and flaps and wings. It takes hours to put it together, and you have to be very good at tying knots, and even better at untying them.

The trouble is that when Dad was putting it together, he made one side heavier than the other, by mistake, so it's always waggling and dipping and turning upside-down in the sky. *He* says it has character.

31

Sometimes, when it's more or less flying, we wander away as if to get a better view of it. And if Dad seems happily occupied, we race off to the playground and stay there until we hear him bawling for help in winding down his awful kite.

Last Sunday we went to Bunch Hill with Dad, to fly the kite for the first time this year. It went up in record time. Our fingers were hardly frozen at all assembling it, and while it was staggering about in the sky we almost forgot it was an hour past lunchtime.

"Look at that," said Dad proudly, "aren't I clever?"

He pointed at the struggling kite. Then the string slipped through his fingers. He grabbed at it, missed and grabbed again as the kite took off, travelling faster and faster, trailing the end of the string along the ground.

We tore after it. "Quick," said Dad, running slowly, "Patrick, Jerry, catch it!"

Just when I could almost snatch the string, the wind filled the kite again and it hurried away. Dad fell over a litter-bin as we ran down Bunch Hill, so he missed the moment when the fleeing kite stalled, twisted in the sky and plunged into the playground, right in front of Banjo the goat.

By the time Dad came limping up, the kite was only a few blue and yellow scraps hanging from Banjo's mouth. Dad was shattered.

"Hours that took me to make, you stupid animal," he shouted at the goat, "hours and hours. Gone in a minute. It's just lunch to you, but it was my lovely kite to me!"

We felt so sorry for Dad that we didn't remind him it was supposed to be *our* kite, not his.

"Let's buy him an ice-cream at Angelo's," said Jerry. We had raspberry-ripple ourselves, and between us we had enough money to bring Dad back a double cone with chocolate flakes. He started licking it moodily.

Then we hopped into a swing-boat and sat idly pulling on the ropes, swinging just a bit. When Dad finished his ice-cream, he still looked miserable.

"Come on, Dad," said Jerry, "no one's looking. We'll give you a ride, it'll cheer you up."

Dad climbed in, and I went and sat at the other end, with Jerry. The balanced weight of the three of us, and Dad's strong pulls made the swing go very fast and high. In a minute the swingboat was bashing against the boughs of the tree, and simply zooming down and up again the other way. It was terrifying.

"Stop!" said Jerry, clutching the side. But Dad was hauling on the rope, watching our end of the swing-boat rocket into the sky. He leaned back to look at the sliding joints of the swing as his own end swooped down and up again among the branches.

"How very interesting," we heard him say.

Jerry was sick.

"Why didn't you tell me you felt sick?" said Dad crossly as we went home. "It must have been all that ice-cream."

Dad spent the afternoon in his garden shed. Soon after that he brought home piles of wood, a big roll of canvas, and buckets and buckets of glue. He measured Jerry and me several times, and he weighed us, separately and together, on the bathroom scales. We really began to worry when he drew the plans for some large, strange, aeronautical object, which seemed to have a kind of boat hanging from it. Then we heard what he was muttering as he crawled about over the enormous plans, his ruler between his teeth.

"Wind force four will carry a boy-lifting kite to a hundred feet in one minute," he was saying.

Jerry and I looked at one another.

"You've gone very pale," said Jerry.

"You've gone rather green," I replied.

"But on the other hand," Dad murmured, staring at his plans, "wind force two might get only half a boy fifty feet in two minutes. This is going to be tricky." And then he looked at us consideringly through half-closed eyes.

But we needn't have worried. Dad finished his new kite, and we flew it from Bunch Hill with the strange boat dangling from it. Jerry and I stared at it glumly.

"It's perfectly safe," said Dad, forgetting that he was holding the kite string, "you just jump in like this, and tug on that rope like that, and – EEEEEAWGH!"

A tremendous gust of wind had struck Bunch Hill. Up went the kite, up went the dangling boat, and up went Dad, over the trees and telegraph poles, his voice growing fainter and fainter as he flew away.

He came down in the boating-lake next to the playground. It was frightfully cold, and he hadn't any oars, of course, and he was covered in duckweed.

I'd better not tell you what he said when we got him out. But I *will* tell you this. Now when we want to go to the playground to see Banjo, or play on the flying-saucer roundabout, we have only to murmur "kites," and Dad puts on his slippers, sits down in his armchair, opens his newspaper and is no bother at all.

The Uncontrollable Octopus

Angela Locke

The uncontrollable octopus lived on the floor of the sea and there he grew enormous. His life was happy enough, catching crabs and shellfish and quietly lurking in underwater caves, until, one day, he felt himself being whisked to the surface and found that he had been caught in a net. It was difficult to tell who was more surprised, the octopus, or Captain Quickdollar and the crew of the fishing boat which had caught him in its trawl nets.

Now the octopus had been very well brought up, and apart from crabs and shellfish he loved every creature he had ever met and even some he had not. So while the Captain and his crew continued to stare very rudely at the octopus, the octopus smiled gently with his beak-like mouth and, squeezing one of his tentacles through the net, placed it tenderly around the shoulders of Captain Quickdollar.

The Captain uttered a strangled cry and his eyes began to pop out of his head. Thinking that the Captain was smiling at him in a charming manner, the octopus squeezed a little harder. At last a brave member of the crew (and there weren't many of those) managed to pull the Captain free, and for a long time he lay on the deck making terrible rasping noises.

The octopus began to feel hurt and neglected, for every time he waved to his new friends they screamed, and ran to the far end of the boat, which tilted alarmingly. He pulled in all his tentacles and sat in a huddle, feeling very uncomfortable in the hot sun.

Meanwhile the Captain was plotting. He decided he could make a lot of money out of the octopus if he sold it to a zoo. So, when the boat docked in the harbour, he sent one of the crew to find the head keeper of the Waterfront Zoo who, Captain Quickdollar thought, would be delighted to buy such an enormous octopus – just as long as he didn't know how uncontrollable it was.

When the head keeper arrived and saw that the Captain had kept the octopus out of the water for so long he was very angry, and rushed off to find a tank for the octopus before it died.

So at last the octopus found himself in a huge, cool aquarium full of sea-water. Oh the wonder and the marvel of it! He did loops and twirls and somersaults, and swallowed lots of water, which he shot out again as he jetted about from one end of the tank to the other.

The head keeper watched him from above. The octopus wanted to say thank you to the keeper for rescuing him so he stretched a tentacle high out of the water and gently pulled him into the tank. Down, down, down, to the bottom of the tank, the uncontrollable octopus lovingly drew the head keeper. But imagine his surprise when the head keeper bonked him on the head. The uncontrollable octopus let go of him rather suddenly and the head keeper shot to the surface, where he lay sobbing until the assistant keepers rescued him.

After that no one was allowed to watch the octopus from the side of the tank, and he grew very lonely. The lions' cage was next door and one day the uncontrollable octopus decided to hook one of the lions over the wall for a chat. Naturally, the lion objected to this and bit the octopus, who squirted inky black stuff all around his tank as octopuses do when they are frightened.

The octopus was then moved into a special tank with very high concrete walls, where the sky seemed a long way away. But the bottom of the tank had been thoughtfully planted with beautiful seaweeds and there were specially built caves in which he could lurk. Now the people could watch him without any danger, because one side of the tank was made of glass and looked over a restaurant. The octopus was rather shy about going near people again after what had happened when he had tried to be friendly before.

But one day he felt so lonely that he decided to swim into the restaurant and say hello to everyone. He couldn't see the sheet of glass which was between him and the people, and he swam straight into it with a terrible sploshing noise. The octopus was very puzzled. He put out all his eight tentacles and pushed hard. The glass started to crack with a loud splintering sound. Water spurted through on to the restaurant floor. There was a lot of screaming and everyone rushed for the door as the tables and chairs and bread rolls started to float about. Finally the whole wall gave way under the weight of the water and the pushing of the octopus. He swam through into the zoo restaurant. It was rather disappointing that everyone had decided to leave, but there was a great deal of delicious food so the octopus settled down for a large meal.

The head keeper was sitting in his office, surrounded by dozens of very wet people from the restaurant, all asking for their money back. He made a sad decision. The uncontrollable octopus would have to go.

The head keeper was a kindly man. He spoke quietly and nicely to Captain Quickdollar who had sold him the octopus. He told him that he expected the octopus to be taken out to sea again and returned to the place where he had been caught. Otherwise the head keeper would ask for his money back.

The Captain turned a nasty shade of green and opened and shut his mouth. But he had to agree, because he had already spent all the money that had been paid to him.

So the uncontrollable octopus was loaded back on to the boat with the help of a net and a crane and taken out to sea. By now he was so upset by the way everyone seemed so frightened of him that all he could do was to sit on his tentacles and feel sad. Very soon he found himself tipped over the side of the boat. Down, down, down he went into the green water until he landed on the sandy bottom.

But then he found he wasn't alone. There, in his favourite spot on a patch of weed, sat a beautiful lady octopus with a shine in her bulging eyes, and gently waving tentacles. The uncontrollable octopus sank down beside her and, very shyly, in case she bit him like the lion, or bopped him on the head like the head keeper, he hesitantly wound his tentacle around her neck. And do you know, I think she rather liked it, for she smiled a beaky smile, and stretching out one of her own tentacles, hugged him right back.

Coba's Birthday Treat

Petronella Breinburg

Not so many years ago, there was a little girl called Coba. Coba lived with her granny and sister Marianne in a village called Para, in a country called Surinam, which is in sunny South America.

In Surinam, there is a capital city, where everyone goes to do their shopping. There are huge ships by the docks, banana boats bobbing along in the river, pretty shops and lots and lots of things to see.

Coba had heard a lot about the city. Her sister had told her, and her granny told her. But Coba had never been to the city. That was because Granny thought that Coba was much too young. The city was busy, the streets full of cars and bicycles. And everywhere there were lots of people pushing.

How Coba longed to see the city. But she wasn't old enough. Then came a very special day, the fifth of April. It was special because, on that day, Coba turned five. She had been asked by Granny what she wanted for her birthday. Coba had said that she would like to go to the city and see the market place. Her granny had agreed.

So, early that April morning, Granny, Marianne and Coba took a train. Even though it was a long train with many carriages it still went fast. It blew and puffed, but sped along, and after a long while they came to the big city. And there, at the station, everyone, including Coba, her sister and her granny, got off the train.

Coba had on her best dress and she felt very proud. She held the wide skirt so that people would see it. But no one looked. Everyone just hurried along the street.

Coba became a little bit frightened. She held on tightly to her granny with one hand and Marianne held her other hand. So fiercely did she clasp Marianne that she said laughingly, "You'll break my hand."

Marianne had been to the city before, she wasn't scared. It was only Coba who kept staring around, just in case one of those hundreds of bicycles or cars should run up and hit them.

They soon came to a huge tower. Coba tilted her head to see

what was on the top. She had just seen that it was a huge clock when it struck with a loud bang. Coba grabbed her sister's hand tighter. She wrinkled up her face. That noise was terrible! Why hadn't her granny warned her that the clocks in the city made such terrible noises?

The people too were noisy. To Coba there seemed to be so *many* people.

"Thousands, hundreds of them," she told Marianne, but Marianne was not listening.

Coba felt terribly hot and her new shoes had begun to pinch.

They then crossed a road and came to a huge market.

"That's not a market," said Coba.

She was very puzzled. The market didn't look like the market she knew in Para. This looked like a long house without its sides, but it had a roof. Coba didn't think that markets had roofs. And there were so many people too. She tried to count them.

"One, two, . . . five, and one more . . . oh!" Coba couldn't count because the people kept moving.

"Look, windmills!" said Marianne.

They were beautiful windmills made from coloured paper.

"Oh! May I have one?" Coba asked. "Oh, please!"

Granny nodded, and then went up to the big boy who was selling the windmills.

"Which one would you like?" The boy bent his head to speak to Coba.

"That one!" Coba pointed to a bright red windmill. She then changed her mind. "No, that one. No, that . . ."

It was Granny who helped Coba to make up her mind. Granny said that other people were waiting to be served, and that they could not stand there all day.

Coba said, "All right," and took a yellow and brown windmill.

The wind began to blow very strongly.

"It's going!" cried Coba, holding the windmill up. "Oh . . ."

Someone had squashed up against Coba. She then had to hold her windmill low down to save it from breaking.

"Put it in my little basket," said Marianne.

"Well . . . well, all right, but I'll carry the basket."

Coba took the basket from Marianne. She then only had one hand left to hold on with. She held on to Granny's hand for a while, but Granny needed two hands to look at the nice clothing and things the city people were selling.

So Coba held onto Granny's koto, which is a huge skirt made up of plenty of lovely cloth.

They were now very squashed and Coba could hardly see anything. Once she tried to peer between her granny and a fat lady, but the lady only came to stand closer to Granny, which blocked Coba's view.

They went to see a man with a monkey. The monkey was doing tricks on a low table and the man was playing a small drum. Round and round the monkey danced. Coba put out her hand. She only wanted to stroke the lovely little monkey, but the man shouted at her. Quickly Coba held on to Granny's koto again.

Suddenly Coba wanted to go home. "There are too many strangers," she thought. She also thought that the people were ill mannered. They didn't ask to get past you the way Granny had taught her to do. Instead they just pushed, and even stepped on other people's feet.

"Granny," said Coba. She wanted to ask if they could go home now.

Her granny did not reply, so Coba tugged hard at the koto. Her granny turned . . . stared.

Coba cried out, "You're not my granny, you're not!" She quickly let go of the koto.

"My granny, Marianne, Grann . . ." Coba wailed.

People stopped to stare. Their faces frightened Coba. They were all strangers. Not one smiled. Not one looked like her granny or like Marianne. Nor did anyone there look like anyone she knew in Para.

Soon Coba had a small circle around her.

"She's lost."

"Granny, Granny . . ." cried Coba.

"She's lost. Get her to the police station."

Someone tried to pick Coba up, but she yelled and kicked. The person quickly put her down. Suddenly Coba heard her sister's voice.

"That's her! That's her!"

"Granny, Granny!" shouted Coba.

"All right, all right, we didn't get far before we missed you," said Granny.

"Ice-cream!" shouted an ice-cream lady. "Get her an ice-cream, poor girl!"

40

Granny did. She got Coba a large ice-cream from the lady, who even put on some extra syrup. Coba began to lick.

Granny held her hand and Coba smiled. She was glad that she had come to the city after all. There was no ice-cream in Para as good as this one and she took a great big lick . . .

"The first of April, some do say"

The first of April, some do say,
Is set apart for All Fools' Day,
But why the people call it so
Nor I nor they themselves do know.

Anon

41

The Littlest Dinosaur

Seona McKinnon

The littlest dinosaur decided that he wanted to be famous.

"What's famous?" asked the Pterodactyl.

"Oh, you know, being the *most* of anything," replied the littlest dinosaur airily, not really quite sure what it did mean.

"The most?"

"Yes. Who is the most frightening dinosaur?"

"Tyrannosaurus Rex, of course."

"Well, then, he is famous because he is the most frightening. But now I am going to be the most frightening dinosaur."

The Pterodactyl just laughed.

"You're only the littlest dinosaur, no one will notice you," he said.

"No one notice me," spluttered the littlest dinosaur in a rage, "no one notice me! I am going to be the most famous, the most frightening dinosaur of all time, in fact I . . ."

"Huh," interrupted the Pterodactyl.

"The biggest, the fiercest . . ." continued the littlest dinosaur coldly.

"But you're not!" argued the Pterodactyl.

"I will be," said the littlest dinosaur, "because I am going to climb to the top of the tallest tree, make my face very, very fierce, and shout frightening noises, then nobody will recognize me. Now, go away, and give me time to make myself fierce, then come back and be frightened."

The Pterodactyl left, and the littlest dinosaur collected leaves and stuck them all over his body with mud. Then he added magnolia flowers in front of his eyes to make them look bigger, and stuck marsh grass on his head for hair.

"Now I am not only the fiercest, but also the hairiest dinosaur in the world. Oh, how famous I will be."

As he climbed the tree he practised the fierce sounds that he would make, and wondered which was the most frightening.

"Tcheeta, tcheeta, groombag, groombag, vablosh, vablosh!"

It was very lonely at the top of the tree, and the littlest dinosaur waited and waited, and tried out a few more fierce sounds.

"Shramblog, shramblog, didrank, didrank."

And he waited and waited.

Then he saw his uncle, the Diplodocus wandering into the clearing below.

"Tcheeta, tcheeta," he shouted.

But the Diplodocus wandered on.

"I suppose that he is becoming a little deaf," thought the littlest dinosaur, "after all he is very old."

The youngest Brontosaurus twins rushed into the clearing. "Vablosh, vablosh!" shouted the littlest dinosaur in his most fierce voice.

But they too rushed on as if they hadn't heard a word.

At last the Pterodactyl came back.

"Groombag, groombag!" shouted the littlest dinosaur as fiercely as he could, but the Pterodactyl didn't even look up.

"Shramblog, shramblog!" the littlest dinosaur screamed, but still the Pterodactyl paid no attention.

The littlest dinosaur was very cross indeed, and he threw down a nut which hit the Pterodactyl on his head. We looked up, saw the littlest dinosaur, and laughed.

"Oh there you are, you *do* look funny."

The littlest dinosaur wasn't pleased and shouted back, "But I'm meant to look fierce."

"Well I think you look funny!" and the Pterodactyl burst out laughing again.

The littlest dinosaur climbed down from the top of the tree, which was not an easy task as his long hair kept catching in the branches.

"Perhaps you could be famous as the smallest dinosaur in the world," suggested the Pterodactyl.

"Don't be silly," snapped the littlest dinosaur. "I'm that already, there's no fun in being what you already are."

Then he had another idea.

"Follow me," he said to the Pterodactyl.

The littlest dinosaur strode through the forest to the edge of the lake. There he found a large rock.

He pushed it but it didn't move. He tried again, and it moved just a little.

"Pterodactyl," he shouted, "come here, can you move this enormous rock?"

The Pterodactyl tried, but the rock didn't move.

"Weakling," scoffed the littlest dinosaur." I can push that rock. I am very strong, in fact, I shouldn't be surprised if I were the strongest dinosaur in the whole world."

"We'll see!" thought the Pterodactyl, and asked the Meganeura, who was flying past, to try to move the rock, but she was not able to push it at all. The littlest dinosaur smiled tolerantly. Then the Pterodactyl asked the Pliosaur to try, but although he was very strong in the waters of the lake where he lived, outside the water he found that he slipped all the time and could not grip the rock.

"See," boasted the littlest dinosaur, "without doubt I am the strongest."

The Pterodactyl was still angry at being called a weakling, and was trying hard to think of someone else who was very strong, when he suddenly noticed the Triceratops triplets in the distance. He rushed over and explained what he wanted them to do. The triplets nodded and ambled over to the littlest dinosaur.

"Pterodactyl says that you think that you are the strongest dinosaur in the world," they said together.

"Oh yes, of course I am," the littlest dinosaur replied. "Look, I can move this huge rock."

And he pushed and pushed, and managed to move it a tiny way along the shore.

"Very good," said the Triceratops, and then they lifted the rock on to their horns and threw it to each other. For a little while they played with the huge rock as if it were no larger than a ball.

At last the littlest dinosaur said sulkily, "Stop. I see you are stronger than I am."

The Triceratops threw the rock around one last time, then started to move away.

"Wait!" shouted the littlest dinosaur in his most determined voice. "Wait. I may not be the fiercest dinosaur, nor the strongest, but I am the cleverest. Look!"

He tucked his head in, and started rolling over and over. He had forgotten that the shore sloped towards the lake, and when he started to turn head over heels he couldn't stop, faster and faster he went, nearer and nearer the lake. He was so busy somersaulting that he didn't hear the animals on the shore laughing, or his mother shouting, "Stop, littlest dinosaur. Stop!"

Splash, splosh! The sudden shock of the icy cold water stopped him.

44

All the animals who had gathered on the shore roared with laughter.

"Ugh!" said the littlest dinosaur as he wiped the water out of his eyes, and shook his ears, "Ugh, what a surprise!"

"I don't think that was very clever," said his mother, "it was . . ."

"Very funny," interrupted the Brontosaurus, "very, very funny!"

"In fact," added the Tyrannosaurus Rex, "I think that you are the funniest dinosaur in the world."

"Yes, yes," said the other animals, still laughing.

The littlest dinosaur looked at the water dripping from his feet, and smiled contentedly. He was the funniest dinosaur in the world. Perhaps he would be famous after all.

The Ant, the Spider and the Caterpillar

Arthur Scholey

It was a fine, blustery, spring day. The wind was shaking the tree's branches, and even blowing one or two leaves into the stream below. But fat, furry Caterpillar munched on; she was relieved to see that her leaf was still firmly fixed, and there was nothing else to be done but gobble, gobble, gobble, while there was still time.

"Good day to you, Caterpillar!" a tiny voice cried. Caterpillar gulped, her jaws working on a juicy piece, "Oh, excuse me – mouth's full . . . good day to you." She peered down. "But what *are* you? Can you possibly be an ant?"

"That's right."

"Then what are you doing up here?"

"Feeling rather giddy, Caterpillar, at the moment. I wish this leaf would keep still."

Caterpillar longed to gobble on, but Ant stayed put.

"Er, shouldn't you be in your ant-hill, or wherever it is you little fellows live?" hinted Caterpillar.

Ant came near, clinging carefully to the leaf.

"I should, yes," he replied. "But, you see, we ants have decided to move on. There are so many disturbances. Humans, and animals, and creatures of all kinds, seem fascinated by our ant-hill. So the ants sent me to find a new home. I climbed this tree to see if I could spot a nice quiet place on the bank further down the stream."

"Well, Ant, you can't look out from *this* leaf," said Caterpillar. "I'm just about to finish gobbling it up, before the wind blows it away. So . . ."

But now there was a further interruption. Sliding down from the leaf above came Spider.

"Excuse me, Caterpillar!"

"Oh dear, trouble!" she sighed.

"Trouble? Not at all," said Spider, landing neatly.

"We spiders are the most peaceable creatures, provided we get co-operation, of course and – oh, oh!" said Spider, looking round, "is that an ant? Not much flesh on ants but they're quite tasty."

"What do you want, Spider?' said Caterpillar hurriedly.

Spider turned back to her.

"I want this leaf," he said. "I need an extra place to fix my new web, and this is ideal. As soon as the wind stops I'll start work. So if you wouldn't mind?"

"I *do* mind, Spider. I've just got the taste of this one."

"And I, my fat friend," said Spider, with new menace in his voice, "I think I could get a taste for *you*, particularly after nibbling this ant for starters."

Whoosh! There was a sudden gust of breeze. The leaf was lifted up into the air and away it went turning over and over, whirling round and down, down to the stream.

"What's happening?" gasped Caterpillar.

"The leaf broke off!" shouted Ant.

"I know that, but where are we now?"

"We appear," said the spider in a matter-of fact voice, "to have landed in the stream."

"Oh dear," sighed Caterpillar, "and *he's* still with us!"

"Very much so, my dear friends," said Spider, spinning a few threads to hang on to.

"Hold on!" warned Ant as the leaf reared up high on a wave and then plunged them down the other side showering them with water.

"I can't stand it!" cried Caterpillar. "What's that banging, that awful jolting?"

"We're colliding with the bank, and bouncing off the rocks in the middle of the stream," Ant explained.

"I do wish the leaf would stop going round and round. I'm quite dizzy," moaned Caterpillar.

Spider had finished his spinning. He clung on to the threads.

"There! Now I feel more secure," he said. He turned to Ant and Caterpillar. "My friends, legend has it that at the end of this stream there is something known as the Waterfall, which is doom for all creatures."

"What a comfort you are, Spider," cried Caterpillar. "However, if we *are* doomed, I might as well spend the last few minutes as best I can."

"What are you doing, Caterpillar?" Ant called out in alarm.

"Mmm, finishing off this juicy leaf, of course! What else is there to do?"

"You mustn't! You're eating our boat."

"Can't help that. It's delicious!"

"But we'll all drown!"

47

"Stop, Caterpillar, at once! "Spider demanded. "If anyone's going to do some eating, I am. The two of you will be enough food for me as long as the journey lasts. I'll start with you, Ant."

"But if this Waterfall thing is at the end of it, what's the point?" asked Ant. "Surely, between us, we can think of a way to escape?"

"Mmm, I can't, Ant," said Caterpillar, happily munching. "I'm too busy enjoying this."

"And I'm getting more and more hungry every second!" warned Spider.

"Help! Big rock ahead. Right in our way. Look out!" cried Ant.

There was a tremendous crash, an enormous swirl of the leaf, another crash – and once more they were back in midstream.

Then, a gasping voice was heard.

"Help! Help me!"

"It's Spider! He's overboard!" cried Ant. Spider was struggling in the torrent, his legs waving wildly.

"Help!" he pleaded. "I'm going under."

"Good riddance!" sniffed Caterpillar. "It could have been me in the water, but I've more legs than he has. I can cling better."

Ant scuttled to the edge of the leaf.

"Look! He's still hanging on by one of his threads. We can't let him drown."

"Yes, we can," said Caterpillar with a smirk.

"If you hold me, Caterpillar, I could help to pull him in."

"You *do* realize he was about to gobble us both up?" Caterpillar was astonished at Ant's suggestion.

"Help!" came another, but much weaker, cry.

"Hold on to me, Caterpillar, *please*."

"I just don't understand it," said Caterpillar. Then with a shrug, "Well, here goes. I'll cling on to you. You pull on the thread."

"Thanks, Caterpillar. Hang on, Spider," Ant called out. "We'll soon have you back on board."

Spider was now sinking but he still clung on to the last thread. Ant heaved on it while Caterpillar spread herself, firmly fixing her many legs and holding fast to Ant.

"Spider!" cried Ant, "*you* must pull as well."

"I'm trying," answered Spider weakly.

Eventually he reached the leaf. Two legs clutched the side.

"That's it! One more heave!"

And he collapsed, gasping but safe, on the leaf.

"Oh . . . thank you, thank you."

"We're hitting the bank!" Ant shouted.

There was a banging and a shuddering jolt. The leaf swept round and out into midstream again.

"I really can't take any more," moaned Caterpillar.

"I've got an idea!" Ant yelled excitedly.

Caterpillar groaned.

"How are you feeling, Spider?" asked Ant.

"Very weak," sighed Spider, spinning a thread to fasten himself to the leaf.

"Now listen. Suppose, the next time we come near the bank, you made a jump for it, with your thread still fastened to the leaf. And you could then pull from the bank, while we do the same from the leaf."

Ant stopped. There was a roaring sound.

"What's that? Listen," he said.

Spider lifted his head and listened.

"It must be the waterfall!" he whispered.

"You must jump, Spider, "Ant cried in a frenzy of excitement. "Now! Look we're nearing the bank again. Jump! Before it's too late."

Spider made a desperate leap for the bank. The thread billowed out behind him.

"He's landed! Hang on, Caterpillar," Ant shouted. "Hang on! Any second now there's going to be an awful jolt!"

And an awful jolt it was, too. The thread stretched and pulled the leaf, almost sending Ant and Caterpillar slipping off into the stream. Somehow they held on.

"Now, start pulling," Ant cried. "Come on, Caterpillar, *pull*! I knew we could do it, if we worked together."

As they both pulled and pulled, Caterpillar asked, between gasps, "What happens when we land? Once the emergency is over?"

Ant looked at Caterpillar.

"Yes, I think we'd better make sure we know what we're doing. You're absolutely right, Caterpillar."

On the bank, straining and struggling, Spider did his best to wind in the thread.

"I'm not certain . . . I can hold on . . . much longer," he groaned. "And, anyway, now that *I'm* safe why should I bother about those two?"

"Keep pulling, Spider, we're nearly in, "Ant's voice called from the leaf.

"On the other hand," said Spider to himself, still pulling, "they did help me when I nearly drowned, so perhaps, yes, I will help them."

"Heave! heave! heave!" Both Ant and Caterpillar's voices were getting louder.

"And, of course, if it hadn't been for Ant's idea in the first place, I suppose I wouldn't be safe on the bank myself. And what's more, after all this exertion and excitement, I'm more hungry than ever. And here, on this leaf, though they don't know it, is my dinner!"

The leaf touched the bank. Ant and Caterpillar scrambled on to dry land.

Spider beamed at them both.

"Well, now," he said, rubbing his two front legs together, "we ought to celebrate our escape, don't you think? While I was pulling you in I noticed, just here in this tree trunk – see, here it is – a nice dry comfortable hole. If you would care to wait in here, my friends, I will go and find us a few tasty flies and . . ."

He turned back, and stopped. Ant and Caterpillar were nowhere to be seen.

"Caterpillar? Ant? Where are you?" he called. "Where are you, where are you . . ."

Ant watched from their hiding-place behind the tree.

"He's going. Don't move just yet, Caterpillar. You were right, though. He *was* going to gobble us both up."

"I could see it in his eyes," said Caterpillar. "After all we've been through together. It was different when we were in danger, but what a nasty creature he still was underneath. And what a juicy leaf that is, just there . . . mmm . . . mmm."

"Well, good-bye, Caterpillar," said Ant. It was a long way back to the ant-hill.

"Oh . . . are you going? Mm . . . mmm . . . even juicier . . . than the other one . . . mmm . . . mmm . . .," said Caterpillar, pausing only briefly between munches. "Funny little fellow, really. I suppose these ants do have *some* purpose? . . . mmm . . . mmm . . . absolutely delicious!"

May

The May Tree

When Maytime's in
  the meadowside,
    the Hawthorn tree
      becomes a bride!

From top to toe
  in perfect dress
    she   dazzles me
      with loveliness –

White gloves, white veil
  all country-sweet,
    with white confetti
      at her feet.

Norah Hussey

Merry May

The sky scowls,
The wind howls,
The leaves shrivel up in folds;
  The flocks and herds
  And little birds
Are all suffering from colds:
  And my nose
  Is quite froze!
With teeth chattering away,
  Let us sing
  Severe Spring,
O miserable May!

Percival Leigh

51

May Queen

Jean Watson

"Hi, mum!" called Jo, slamming the front door behind her.

"Hullo, dear!" said her mother. "Had a good day?"

"No work!" gloated her daughter. "We spent all day getting ready for the festival."

"Have they chosen the May Queen yet?" her mother asked.

The expression in Jo's dark eyes changed – just for a second. Then she tossed her head and replied, making her voice light and casual, "Yep. It's Laura Barton, of course."

In case her mother should offer unwanted sympathy, she added, quickly, "Who would want to be a May Queen, anyway?" before thundering upstairs to change out of her school uniform.

In her bedroom, she stood and stared at her reflection in the long mirror. Brown eyes, short, curly brown hair, small face, small nose, small ears. Small everything, she thought disgustedly.

Never in a million years would anyone choose her for the May Queen. So why had she been dumb and stupid enough to keep hoping that they would? It was obvious that Laura Barton, with her long golden hair and blue eyes was made for the part. All the same, disappointment swept over Jo again. How she had hoped that, just this once, she'd be the one sitting on the flower-decked throne, wearing the white dress and the crown of carnations! She blinked back the tears and turned away.

When she had changed, she went downstairs and straight out into the garden. Her mother, seeing her move slowly down the path, smiled fondly. She knew her daughter's need to be alone in the garden straight after a day of school.

Jo walked slowly to the bottom of the garden where the grass grew long, and wild flowers added gentle splashes of colour. Then she lay down, with her hands behind her head, and gazed at the drifting clouds. Yet even here, in her favourite place, and even now, in her favourite moment of the day, she kept thinking of Laura Barton.

Jo closed her eyes and made a great effort to blot out all her thoughts and feelings. Presently, a drowsy warmth filled her from head to toe . . .

52

The voice was so tiny that she thought she must have imagined it. But when she opened her eyes and turned her head, she knew that she hadn't. For there was a grasshopper, standing an inch from her nose, and repeating his question in a high, reedy voice.

"May I have the pleasure of this dance?"

"Dance!" echoed Jo, hurriedly sitting up and looking round. The sight which met her eyes brought a gasp of astonishment and pleasure from her. Behind the grasshopper, and inside a circle of grass bordered by wild flowers, waltzed insects of all shapes, colours and sizes. There were ladybirds, crickets, grasshoppers, caterpillars, worms, spiders and many different kinds of beetle.

Above the sound of their whispering voices, Jo could now hear sweet, rippling, bubbling music – like a harp being played by the wind.

A strange excitement filled her and turning back to her companion she said, "I would love to dance, but how can I? What a giant I must seem to be!"

"You can easily change that by drinking from the cups of seven bluebells," he replied.

Jo turned to look again at the ring of wild flowers which outlined the ballroom area. Among the scarlet pimpernel, yellow primroses and purple dog-violets, a bluebell glowed like a cluster of sapphires. Delicately, she picked one tiny, fragile cup and lifted it to her lips.

The liquid which trickled from it on to her tongue tasted like honey, but it was neither as sticky nor as thick. After draining the seventh cup, she felt as though she were travelling very fast, but she was not in the least frightened. When that feeling had passed, she looked around.

"I must be in the jungle!" she thought, then quickly realized that the tall green spears around her were only grass blades and that she was now a little shorter than the grasshopper.

"Come," he said, holding out an arm. She took it and they joined the other dancers.

Jo tripped, swayed, skipped, hopped and whirled with one delightful insect-companion after another. Then strong, beautiful chords were heard and in the silence which followed them a clear voice announced, "And now the time has come for us to crown our queen!"

The insects moved back to form an aisle. Down this came a procession bearing flowers. First were the ladybirds with a crown of kingcups. To Jo's amazement, they stopped directly in front of her. The next instant she found herself crowned with the lovely flowers.

Then the beetles led her to a chair, made of twigs and leaves, and covered with petals of all shades. In this she was carried round the bottom of the garden, and each blade of grass and flower bowed as she passed.

Afterwards, her throne was placed in the centre of the grass circle. From this position she watched the insects performing. First the ladybirds marched in formation, making wonderful patterns as they moved. Then the grasshoppers and crickets sang and played their musical instruments. They were followed by some morris-dancing beetles, waving leaves instead of handkerchiefs, and some acrobatic caterpillars, worms and spiders, who did fantastic wriggling and climbing acts.

Finally, one of each kind of insect was chosen to dance round the maypole, which was a twig placed firmly in the ground. The streamers were goose-grass and willow tips, interlaced with flowers. Watching this colourful skipping dance, Jo began to feel as though she were sinking down, down, down into a sea of all the most beautiful and pleasing sounds, colours and smells. It was a delightful sensation, and she closed her eyes with a happy sigh . . .

When she opened them she was life-size again, lying on the grass and covered with apple blossoms. Nothing was left to remind her of what had just happened, except a grasshopper, an inch from her nose, and a warm, drowsy feeling of contentment.

Slowly she got up and wandered back to the house, remembering the school May Queen without a single pang; remembering, too, every detail of the music, the dancing, the acrobatics and the flowers, and picturing her tiny, loyal subjects. What a coronation it had been!

"It may not *sound* much to be Queen of the Bottom of the Garden," thought Jo, "but, oh, it's a thousand times better than being the school May Queen, if they did but know it. But they don't and they never will, because it's my secret."

Going into the kitchen, she heard her mother talking on the hall telephone.

"Always has done," she was saying. "Straight after school. Goes right round the garden. Just as though she were checking over her own kingdom."

Jo stood still, listening. "Checking over her own kingdom." The words pleased her. Then she went into the hall.

Seeing her daughter, Jo's mother hurriedly ended her conversation and put down the phone. Then she noticed Jo's secret-hugging smile and said, "You look like the cat that's swallowed the cream!"

And Jo replied, "If only you knew!"

Simply-Wonderful and Perfectly-Foul

Margaret Cooper

Once upon a time there were two men who lived in the same little town. In a house at the top of the town lived Augustus, but everyone called him Simply-Wonderful. In a house at the bottom of the town there was Ernest, but everyone called him Perfectly-Foul.

Sometimes, somewhere in the middle of the town, they passed by each other.

"Good gracious! What a dreary looking specimen," thought one.

"Good grief! What a foolish looking creature," thought the other.

For they were as different as pianos and prunes.

One morning, for instance, Simply-Wonderful bounced out of bed, flung back his curtains and declared to the world, though no one was listening, "What a simply wonderful day! Sunshine and blue skies. A bird-singing, lettuce-sandwich, summer-clothes day."

He hummed loudly through his exercises, threw on his shorts and tee-shirt and set off with an eager stride.

But when the clouds, which he hadn't noticed before, blotted out the sunshine patches, it grew distinctly chilly. People began to snigger at his knees, which had turned blue, and at his arms, which were smothered in goosepimples. When his teeth began to chatter he decided it was time to go home and get warm.

Perfectly-Foul, on the other hand, looked just as daft that day. He got out of bed and peered gloomily at the sky.

"It's going to rain," he pronounced, seeing only the clouds. "Another perfectly foul day."

He carefully put on his wellington boots, struggled into a heavy rubber mackintosh, fastened a huge sou'wester tightly under his chin and plodded off to the bread shop.

"Where's your boat, mister?" children shouted and, "Look out! Moby Dick's behind you."

And it didn't rain. Every time the sun came out Perfectly-Foul thought he would melt. He arrived home as red as a beetroot and feeling like an over-soggy sponge.

The next morning both men awoke to find it was raining, bucketing down from a grim-grey sky.

Simply-Wonderful was thrilled to bits.

"Oh, to feel those divinely refreshing droplets on my face!" he cried and straight away rushed off down the road. "Enchanting day!" he announced beamingly to puzzled passers-by. "Just think," he enthused to no one in particular, "all around us flowers and trees are drinking up the rain, growing tall and strong. And raindrops are dancing on rivers and lakes. Oh, it's too poetic," he concluded, wringing his hands with a simply wonderful flourish.

But it wasn't poetic enough. When he got home there were pools of water under all the windows as he had forgotten to shut them before he left. And in his garden shed there was a positive flood for he had never got around to mending the hole in the roof. He spent the whole evening wringing out wet carpets, soggy rugs and cold, damp bedspreads. He crawled into bed exhausted.

Perfectly-Foul, on the other hand, groaned when he saw the rain.

"Nasty, beastly stuff! Puddles everywhere. Mud all over the place. Perfectly foul!" he complained. And instead of going to the shops he spent the entire day making sure not even the tiniest spot of rain got into his house.

He closed all the windows. He filled up every single crack and gap and hole he could find. He nailed planks of wood to his shed roof to make doubly certain his tools kept dry. And he put a new lock on his kitchen door so that it shut much more firmly. Finally, he bolted his front door and flopped into his armchair. His house was completely watertight. He was satisfied.

But five minutes later he was not nearly so satisfied. It was after six, the shops had closed and he had no food. So Perfectly-Foul went to bed that night beautifully dry and horribly hungry.

Later that year when the snow fell Simply-Wonderful threw open his bedroom window and inhaled excitedly.

"So enchanting! So unspoilt!" he marvelled. "A sparkling whiteness not to be missed."

He pulled on some woolly clothes and made straight for the park. He spent the morning skating on the frozen lake and sledging down the snow-thick slopes. Eager not to miss any of the fun, he gulped down some hot soup in the park cafe and rushed back to the snowball fights.

But there was not much fun when he got home. Stuck through

his letter-box were two angry notes. His aunty had struggled through the heavy snow to deliver a chocolate cake which she baked him every week. Finding that his front path was dangerously slippery and his side door blocked by a snowdrift, she had taken the cake back home.

"I probably won't ever make you another one," her note said.

The milkman had also called. He had done his best to leave the milk. But he'd lost his balance on the treacherous surface, performed a spectacular somersault and crashed to the ground, bottles and all.

"If you can't be bothered to clear your paths, mate," his note ended, "I can't be bothered to deliver your milk."

"And I can't be bothered delivering your letters," the postman had added underneath.

"And I can't be bothered bringing your bread," the breadboy had written underneath that.

Of course, Perfectly-Foul had a very different day. Just looking at all that snow depressed him, for snow meant hard work. He solemnly set about clearing every inch from his front path (in case someone called at his front door), then from his side path (in case someone called at his side door) and finally from his back garden (in case anyone called at his back door). And because he was always more than thorough he cleared half the road as well.

He shovelled and scraped all day and when at last he sat down for his tea he was frozen to the marrow. He spent the next week in bed, sneezing, coughing, aching and groaning.

One blazing hot summer's afternoon, Simply-Wonderful and Perfectly-Foul, rather surprizingly, bumped into each other.

Perfectly-Foul usually kept out of the sun for he was sure it was bad for his health. But on this particular day he had an urgent letter to post and, covering as much of himself as he possibly could, he made a dignified dash for the post office. Simply-Wonderful, on the other hand, had been sauntering around for hours in shorts and bare feet.

Both men looked as they passed each other. Then both stopped and turned around.

"I say," ventured Simply-Wonderful, "you look awfully pale. You should get out more. Get some fresh air and sun. Just look at all those clothes you've got on."

"And just look at all those clothes you haven't got on!" retorted Perfectly-Foul. "You're a sight for sore eyes. You should be indoors in this heat. Still," he added, "you never have had any sense."

"And you know your trouble," chided Simply-Wonderful, "you're much too careful. Never seem to enjoy yourself."

The two went on flinging rude remarks at each other – until they just couldn't think of any more. Neither spoke for a minute. Then Simply-Wonderful, looking unusually thoughtful, said, "Er . . . what about sharing a house?"

"Sharing a house!" gasped Perfectly-Foul, shocked at the very idea.

Then gradually, *very* gradually, he began to smile – a little.

"Yes," he said slowly. "That could be a good idea."

So that's what they did. They agreed to share a house.

Happy-go-lucky Simply-Wonderful got a bit more organized, which was not a bad thing. And cautiously, careful Perfectly-Foul got a bit less organized, which was not a bad thing either.

It all worked out surprisingly well, in fact.

Now, for instance, on very hot days Simply-Wonderful no longer sleeps in the sun all day, burning himself to a cinder. Perfectly-Foul no longer hides behind drawn curtains growing pale and uninteresting. Instead, at the suggestion of Simply-Wonderful, they spend an hour together in the sun. Then, on the recommendation of Perfectly-Foul, they retire indoors for an hour. Later, at the insistence of Simply-Wonderful, they are out in the sunshine again. Later still, on orders from Perfectly-Foul, they are cooling off inside the house. So in summer they are neither too pale nor too burnt. Just a lovely golden brown.

To be absolutely honest, there are still the odd occasions when the two go back to their old ways. You can see Perfectly-Foul clutching a raincoat and umbrella on the hottest June day and Simply-Wonderful sporting open-toed sandals in the snowy depths of January. But that's not such a bad thing, is it?

June

A Hot Day

Cottonwool clouds loiter.
A lawnmower, very far,
Birrs. Then a bee comes
To a crimson rose and softly,
Deftly and fatly crams
A velvet body in.
A tree, June-lazy, makes
A tent of dim green light.
Sunlight weaves in the leaves,
Honey-light laced with leaf-light,
Green interleaved with gold.
Sunlight gathers its rays
In sheaves, which the wind unweaves
And then reweaves – the wind
That puffs a smell of grass
Through the heat-heavy, trembling
Summer pool of air.

A. S. J. Tessimond

Traffic Jam

Roar-roaring
Engines running
Horns hooting
Brakes grinding
Gears grating
Rev-revving
Creep, creeping
Overheating
Long waiting
Traffic jam.

Anne English

The Lion Watch

Gwen Grant

Indani the lion smelt danger. He lifted his head sharply and his glowing yellow eyes swept over the open plain. A long way away he saw dust clouds. As he watched, a large animal stopped, and the dust settled back into the earth. The beast did not come too close.

This was a strange animal. It smelt like no animal Indani knew. It made a loud grumbling noise, as if it were angry.

Indani stiffened. This was his territory. He lived on this piece of the plain. The strange animal in front of him must be made to go.

But, before the lion had a chance to move, the animal stopped growling and shaking from side to side. It stood still under the hot African sun.

Out of the strange beast climbed another animal. Indani sniffed the air. He knew what this creature was. He had seen it before. The lion stared unblinkingly at the man who had stepped out of his Landrover. Indani remembered the last time he had seen such a creature. It had a long stick. When it pointed the stick at the beasts who lived on the plains, the stick made a loud noise. "Bang! Bang!" it went and animals fell to the ground. They never moved again.

Stealthily the lion moved back into the cover of the bushes around him. In the bushes were his family. A pride of six lions. There was Neeka the lioness and mother of the three lion cubs, and there was Goan, sister of Neeka.

Goan had no cubs. She helped Neeka. Goan looked on Neeka's cubs as her own.

Indani padded through the bush to his family. He coughed and rumbled at Neeka and Goan, telling them of the two legged beast which walked the plains.

"Danger!" Indani growled. Danger from the long stick.

Neeka looked round for her cubs. Two were missing. She grunted to Goan. "The cubs are gone."

Neeka swept through the long grass. Goan padded behind her. The cubs were playing. They were racing round and round, pulling each other's tails. Biting each other's ears.

Neeka moaned at them loudly. The sound echoed through the

61

plain. Man the hunter turned his head. He listened for the lioness to call her children once more.

But Neeka had no need to call again. At the first moan, the cubs tumbled towards their mother. Towards Goan, sister of Neeka, second mother to the lion children.

Goan was to take the cubs to safety. Neeka would not leave Indani. Goan hid the lion children. The cubs lay still. Goan lay in front of them. As soon as her long heavy body touched the ground, she could not be seen. Goan was the colour of dark honey. The same colour as the plain.

The black lines on Goan's ears shaded her head into the grass. Only Neeka would see the watchful yellow eyes. Only Indani would smell Goan was there.

But danger! Danger! The hunter was walking towards Goan. Indani made ready to face the creature with the long stick.

The lion dropped his head, bringing his tail stiffly into the air. He tensed. Those gleaming eyes scorched the plain in front of him. He roared. The hunter stood still. The sound of the lion told him he should not go closer. He stepped back. To the side of him, Neeka emerged from the bush.

The hunter's eyes followed her. Neeka was more dangerous than Indani. The lioness is always fiercer than the lion.

Behind the hunter, the Landrover roared into life.

Indani watched the big animal creeping closer and closer. The man in the Landrover switched on the headlights. They burned in the bright sunny air. Indani watched these round white eyes. They were not the eyes of Neeka. Nor the eyes of Goan. These were eyes the colour of the sun.

The Landrover stopped again. Neeka crouched on the dry grass. Slowly, she started to move. She swung out into a curve. Indani waited. He did not move. He did not take his eyes off man the hunter.

He waited until the time Neeka had the hunter trapped between herself and Indani.

The hunter knew about lions. He moved backwards. Back to the safety of the Landrover. Now Neeka moved faster too. The hunter turned his back on Indani and ran to the Landrover.

Indani watched the running animal. He was tired. He was angry. With a roar he leapt forward. The hunter turned his head. He saw Indani coming towards him very fast. He knew lions could run fifty yards in two seconds.

As the hunter turned his head, he tripped. He lay on the hot earth. "Help me!" he shouted.

The driver of the Landrover sent it racing over the plains towards the hunter. There was no time to lose. Indani had nearly reached his prey. Neeka was closing in from the right.

The Landrover didn't stop until it stood over the hunter's body. The hunter scrambled from underneath it and threw himself through the open door of the Landrover – to safety.

Indani growled angrily. He stood still, lashing his tail. Neeka waited to see what he would do next. Then, she heard the mewl of a cub.

"Danger! Danger!" Neeka rumbled to Indani.

The lion and lioness turned. A cub was out on the plain. It had slipped away from Goan's care. A pack of hyenas were slinking towards it. Neeka moaned loudly. The cub turned towards its mother. The hyenas paused, then sent one of their pack after the cub. "Quick. Quick," they called.

Neeka moved swiftly but Goan was there before her. Goan snarled, ready to attack but the hyena fled. Goan chased the cub back to its hiding place. She looked longingly after the spotted, dog-like animal with its short hind legs and sloping back but she would not leave Neeka's cubs.

The Landrover started its engine, breaking the silence of the plain, putting the pack of hyenas to flight, stopping Neeka in her pursuit.

The hunter leant out of the window and pointed a black shape at the lions and then at the vanishing hyenas. He pressed a lever. Click! Click! it went. The animals did not fall to the ground. For this was a hunter of pictures. A hunter with a camera, not a gun. The Landrover pulled back. A long way back from the lions.

Indani waited. Then he shook his heavy mane and turned away. He yawned hugely. He called his family to his side. Neeka came. The three cubs came. Goan, sister of Neeka, second mother to the cubs came. The pride of lions were together once more.

The plains settled into silence.

How the Tortoise got his Cracks

An African story retold by Gladys Williams

Once upon a time, before there were any people, and animals had the world to themselves, a tortoise and his family lived happily on a sunny hillside. Tortoises in those days had nice, smooth, shiny shells on their backs, without a single bump or crack, so that they could use each others shells for looking-glasses.

One spring there was no rain. And then came the summer sun ten times hotter than usual, and presently all the plants and grass began to die and soon there was nothing at all to eat. The tortoise and his wife and children got hungrier and hungrier, and he just didn't know what to do.

So the tortoise said to his family one morning, "Let us all go out in different directions and look for something to eat."

So off they all set, each going a different way. The tortoise took a little basket and walked towards the forest hoping to find, perhaps, a few berries that had not been dried up by the sun. But nowhere could he find a single fruit of any kind. He felt so weak and hungry he didn't know what to do.

And then, coming towards him down the forest path he saw a big bird, a quail. Now the quail didn't look at all thin or tired like all the other animals. In fact it looked just as if times were as usual and there wasn't any famine.

The tortoise looked and looked at the bird and he thought, "That bird's getting food from somewhere. Perhaps I can creep quietly behind him and find out where."

But when the quail came right up to him he stopped and said, "Hallo, brother. How are you? You look rather thin and tired."

"Oh I am," said the tortoise. "I've had hardly anything to eat for a week and I am very hungry. And I'm tired, too, because I've been searching all the morning for some food to take home to my dear wife and two small children. But see, my basket is still quite empty."

"Oh dear," said the quail in a kindly voice, "that's very sad, but perhaps I can help you. I get fed each day, and if you come with me I will show you how I manage it."

This was better than the tortoise had dared hope. He thanked the quail over and over again, and began to follow him through the forest.

The quail led him to a great, tall, stately tree, whose roots went deep into the earth and whose branches stretched up nearly to the sky; and the branches of the tree were covered in beautiful fruit. But they were all far too high for the tortoise to reach.

But that didn't seem to worry the quail.

"How many are there in your family?" he asked.

"Four," said the tortoise.

"Ah yes," said the quail, and looking up at the great tree he spoke to it. "Tree," he said, "send down four fruits, please."

And the tree did! Four lovely fruits dropped to the ground just in front of the tortoise – fruits like little coconuts, providing both food and drink.

The tortoise was amazed and delighted.

"Put them in your basket and go home to your family," said the quail. "You may come back to my tree and ask for four fruits each day, tomorrow and the day after that, and the day after that, as long as the famine lasts."

Again the tortoise thanked the quail and then hurried off home with his prize.

But directly he was inside his own front door, he gobbled down his fruit as fast as he could. Then he found a great big clothes-basket, the biggest one in all the house, and hurried back to the tree, with it. On the way he wondered if he would be able to find the tree and if it would still have its branches covered with fruit.

He found the tree without any difficulty and gazed up at its great branches laden with fruit. Would the tree obey him as it obeyed the quail? He stood right under it and looked up at it and he said, "Tree, send down four *thousand* fruits."

And the tree *did*! It shook its branches and the tortoise tried to run away as the fruits came crashing down on top of him. And that is why all the descendants of the tortoise, right to this very day, have such cracked-looking, bumpy shells, and have to *buy* looking-glasses if they need them.

Rain in Summer

How beautiful is the rain!
After the dust and heat,
In the broad and fiery street,
In the narrow lane,
How beautiful is the rain!

How it clatters along the roofs,
Like the tramp of hoofs!
How it gushes and struggles out
From the throat of the overflowing spout!

Across the window-pane
It pours and pours;
And swift and wide,
With a muddy tide,
Like a river down the gutter roars
The rain, the welcome rain.

The sick man from his chamber looks
At the twisted brooks;
He can feel the cool
Breath of each little pool;
His fevered brain
Grows calm again,
And he breathes a blessing on the rain.

From the neighbouring school
Come the boys,
With more than their wonted noise
And commotion;
And down the wet streets
Sail their mimic fleets,
Till the treacherous pool
Engulfs them in its whirling
And turbulent ocean.

In the country, on every side,
Where far and wide,

Like a leopard's tawny and spotted hide,
Stretches the plain,
To the dry grass and the drier grain
How welcome is the rain!

Henry Wadsworth Longfellow

Crab's Kingdom

Tessa Morris-Suzuki

In the beginning there was a rock pool.

It was older than human memory. Year after year the sea had worn away at the rocks until the pool was a smooth hollow. When the tide came in, the pool became shadowy and mysterious. When the tide went out it became a shining basin of clear water. It never overflowed and never became dry.

The pool was a kingdom of its own. If you looked into its depths you could see many living things: fish and starfish, silent limpets and lively hermit crabs, shrimps and sea anemones. And sometimes, if you watched carefully, you could see a creature with a fine shell of mottled brown and white.

That was Crab, the king of the rock pool.

Like most kings, Crab had a rather good life.

He had long legs and sharp pincers. He could run faster than any other creature in the pool. He was the strongest animal in his kingdom, and he could not help being rather proud.

He lived in a dark hole under a ledge of rock. Near his stronghold the pool was shallow and its floor was flat and sandy. But at the other end, where the water was deeper, a forest of feathery weeds grew right up to the gateway which led into the open sea.

Sometimes, when the weather was stormy, the tide would wash some strange creature into the pool, but usually life in the pool was peaceful. Tides rose and fell, bringing in food and fresh water. The sun shone by day. At night the pool gleamed under the dark sky.

At least, that was how things were until the day when the invasion began . . .

It began like any other day. The first specks of sunlight touched the pool. The Crab went out of his stronghold and felt the swirl of water around him. The tide was coming in. It was time to go hunting.

The Crab set off toward the forest. On his way he greeted the quiet contented limpets and the hermit crabs which scuttled about in their funny top-heavy shells.

The Crab took a narrow path which led to the depths of the

forest. The tall weeds waved close around him. The sunlight disappeared.

Suddenly the Crab stopped.

In the darkness ahead he could see something strange. It lay near the entrance to the pool. Perhaps it was some unknown enemy from the sea beyond? The Crab gathered his courage and sidled towards the stranger.

It was not like anything he had ever seen before. It was long and shining, almost like a fish, but it was not a fish. It didn't seem to be alive. It drifted on the surface of the pool. It gleamed coldly in the sunlight.

The Thing remained there all day. By the next morning it had sunk to the bottom of the pool. Little by little the creatures in the pool became used to the strange Thing. Soon the hermit crabs were playing around it without fear.

But before long, two more strange Things had appeared in the little kingdom. One was like the first invader. The other was quite different. It was soft and waving, like weed, but it had no colour. It floated round the pool, and at last became stuck in a crack of rock, almost blocking the entrance to Crab's stronghold.

As time went on, more and more strange Things arrived. Some were large and some were small, some hard and some soft. They were all different shapes and colours. Not one of them was alive, but unlike dead things they did not fade and disappear.

The beautiful pool became dirty and crowded.

One day, the Crab climbed out of his pool to lie in the sun. He had just stretched himself out on a dry sandy rock when he noticed a strange sight. A line of hermit crabs was coming out of the pool. When they saw him, they tried to hide.

"Where are you going to?" asked the King Crab.

The hermit crabs shuffled about uncomfortably.

"Well, you see, Your Majesty," said one of them, "we've decided to leave the pool. It used to be a nice clean place, but ever since those strange Things started to appear, the water's been getting dirtier and dirtier. We can't live here any more. We're going to find another pool . . ."

The King Crab was silent. There was nothing he could say. He looked down at his pool. Sure enough, its waters were becoming grey and dirty.

"Go," he said softly. "Go, and I wish you good luck. But I will stay in my pool. Good-bye."

For a long time he stared down at his kingdom, spread out below the smooth, sunny rocks. When he looked round, the hermit crabs had gone. Slowly, Crab crept back into his pool.

The next morning, when Crab left his stronghold, he realized at once that something was seriously wrong.

The tide had stopped. The water was not flowing in from the sea. All was as still as death. Not a ripple stirred in the pool.

Then the Crab saw what had happened. A cluster of strange Things had become wedged among the rocks. They were completely blocking the narrow gateway which joined the pool to the sea beyond.

The Crab was horrified. The tide from the sea was the life-blood of the pool. Without it, how could he find food? How could the water in the pool stay fresh? Already he could feel the murky stillness poisoning his body. He ran to the gateway and tore at the Things with his strong claws, but his grasp slipped on their slimy surface. The Things remained as firmly stuck as ever.

They have won, thought the Crab. They have killed my world. But I have only one kingdom. I cannot leave it. I will stay here until I die.

But if only, he sighed, if only someone could rescue my kingdom . . .

That same morning a boy came to the seashore. He walked barefoot over the rocks.

Now and then he stopped to pick up twisted shells or smooth pebbles. Best of all, he liked to gaze into rock pools. At first he could see nothing in them but sea water and weeds. But then he saw that they were full of life. He saw the darting specks of fishes. He watched anemones slowly changing from blobs of jelly into delicate flowers. It was like discovering a new world.

But the boy found one pool which was not full of life. It was close to a beach which had become covered with rubbish. Picnickers had left empty cans and bottles on the sand. The tide had washed up plastic bags and broken toys.

The waters of this pool were grey and dirty. Nothing seemed to move in them except for evil bubbles which rose to the surface with a plop.

It was Crab's kingdom.

The boy felt sad when he saw the pool. He decided to clean it.

First, with a sharp stick, he fished out all the rubbish which floated on the pool. He cleared its blocked entrance, and he collected all the other litter which was scattered over the rocks and sand.

Then the boy began to dig a pit in the sand. The sun grew hot overhead, but still the boy dug. By noon he had made a deep, dark hole in the beach. He pushed all the rubbish into the hole and covered it with a thick layer of sand.

Next he found some pieces of wood and made large signs. The signs read:

PLEASE DO NOT THROW
YOUR RUBBISH HERE.

He put two signs on the beach and one on the rocks. Then he went home. Darkness gathered above the sea. The inky waves broke over the empty, clean sand and the shining rocks.

The boy went back every day to look at the pool. The tide had begun to flow again. The sea washed away the stagnant water and the dead weeds. But still there seemed to be no life in the pool.

Then on the third day the boy saw something moving. Slowly, a creature appeared from under a ledge of rock. It was a crab. It had a mottled brown and white shell. It moved slowly, as if it was dazed, but even so the boy could see that this was the king of the pool.

To the Crab, it seemed as if it had all been a dream.

The strange Things which had almost killed his kingdom went as they had come, into the unknown.

The tide flowed. Light shone through water. Plants grew again. Slowly, the other creatures returned: the fish, the starfish, the anemones, and last of all the hermit crabs, timidly scuttling back to their old home. In a small corner of the wide sea life began again, almost as if nothing had happened.

Mr Buru-the-Guru and The Flying Mr Mooney

Wendy Wharam

Once upon a time, the world ran out of petrol. There was no petrol to be had anywhere. All along the motorway, cars had stopped. Their tanks were empty. All traffic was at a standstill.

People had to find other ways of getting about. Some went on roller skates some on horseback, on scooters, bicycles, tricycles, pedal-cars and wheel chairs.

The cars were no use to anyone but their owners did not forget them. They were lovingly polished and greased and oiled. Some families made special little shrines so that cars could still be worshipped. Every Sunday they brought flowers, and every fourth Sunday there was a grand parade all around the town. People decorated their cars with garlands and pushed them in the procession.

But the business men, who liked to rush here, there and every-where, were not at all pleased. Without transport, business was bad. They had to do something about it.

One day, ten important business men from the city, in their smart suits and black hats, and one very little, not very important business man called Mr Mooney, knocked on the door of Mr Buru-the-Guru, with the handles of their rolled umbrellas.

Mr Buru-the-Guru, (who was very busy at the time untying the legs of his yoga class, who had got themselves into knots trying to sit in the Lotus position) ushered them in politely.

"Peace be with you, my friends," he said.

The ten business men charged through the door past Mr Buru-the-Guru, fell over their umbrellas, and became entangled with the yoga class.

Mr Buru-the-Guru smiled his peaceful smile at little Mr Mooney, who was standing amazed by the door. The business men picked themselves up, very red in the face, and said loudly, 'We would like you to give us lessons in flying. We can't use our cars any more. We want to get quickly from place to place. Flying is the only answer."

Mr Buru-the-Guru thought for ten minutes. Then he smiled one of his peaceful smiles and said, "Anything is possible. If you wish it, it will be. I charge one hundred pounds fifty pence for flying lessons and prefer payment in advance."

All the business men were very rich. Money was no problem to them, except for little Mr Mooney who had hardly any money at all. But Mr Buru-the-Guru noticed the patch on Mr Mooney's trousers and said he could have the lessons on hire purchase, five pence now and the rest later.

The first lesson took place the next day, in Mr Buru-the-Guru's garden. He asked all the ten business men, and Mr Mooney to sit on the grass and think beautiful thoughts. Before they could think beautiful thoughts, they had to chase away all the ugly thoughts that crowded in.

In some of their heads were dreams of gigantic plates of food – steaks and puddings. Others thought about piles of money and did frantic sums. The numbers went mad in their heads, doing a dance and tumbling over one another. And some dreamed of pretty girls. In Mr Mooney's head was a picture of his fat, lazy wife eating cream cakes they couldn't afford.

"When they were able to think beautiful thoughts," said Mr Buru-the-Guru, "then, and only then, would they be able to think about learning to fly." But it was difficult to sit and think in Mr Buru-the-Guru's garden, for Mr Buru's ten cats perched on the hats of the ten business men as they sat and tried to think beautiful thoughts. So they took off their hats.

Then Mr Buru-the-Guru's ten doves came, billing and cooing, to lay their eggs in the upturned hats of the ten business men.

And then Mr Buru-the-Guru's ten dogs came out barking, chased the cats and the doves, and then there was peace – until ten butterflies came and perched on the noses of the business men and made them sneeze.

"I can see it is difficult here," said Mr Buru-the-Guru. 'We will go to the park."

So the next lesson they all went to the park. They sat on the grass, feeling rather silly. Mr Buru-the-Guru sat with them, not minding, and thinking his beautiful thoughts. But soon the park was full of people. They were all pointing and staring and laughing. So the business men pretended to be reading their newspapers, or began to rush about as though they were looking for

73

something. They didn't want people to think they had come to the park just to think beautiful thoughts.

"This place is not right either," said Mr Buru-the-Guru sadly, taking up his mat.

For the next lesson, they went to the Common. They sat on the top of a hill, where they could see the whole of the city below them.

"Now," said Mr Buru-the-Guru, "we must think of flying. Think of all the things that fly."

So all the business men thought very hard about birds and helicopters and bats and aeroplanes, and flying saucers and butterflies and Jumbo jets.

Mr Mooney thought about the clouds floating up there in the sky, as pale as milk, like great ships sailing in still blue waters. He began to feel like a cloud himself, free and light as air.

He didn't know what had happened to him until he heard a shout, "Look at Mr Mooney. He's flying."

Looking down, he saw the up-turned faces of the ten business men and Mr Buru-the-Guru.

Mr Mooney gave a jaunty wave of his umbrella and landed with a thump at the feet of Mr Buru-the-Guru.

"Pride comes before a fall," said Mr Buru-the-Guru, picking up Mr Mooney and dusting him down.

The other business men were very envious of Mr Mooney and wanted their money back.

"You said you would teach us to fly," they shouted at Mr Buru-the-Guru.

"When you are ready to fly, you will fly," he said to them. "Be at peace."

He explained to them that he couldn't give them their money back because he had given it away. The business men charged down the hill, waving their umbrellas at Mr Buru-the-Guru, but he floated away serenely in the sky, like a great white bird, smiling his peaceful smile.

He was following the trail of little Mr Mooney – flying home to tea and crumpets.

The Trail of a Snail

Ruth Ainsworth

There was once a family of baby snails, who lived under a cabbage leaf with their mother. They thought the sheltering green leaf was the whole world, but their mother told them, when they were older, she would show them many wonderful things in other parts of the garden.

"But," she said, "there are dangers waiting for little snails; hungry birds, and gardeners who wish that snails had never been invented. I will teach you how to keep safe and live long, active lives."

"I want to explore the garden now," said Humpy, who was a naughty little snail. "I can look after myself."

"Wait until you are bigger," said his mother, "then you can be a great explorer like your father. Why, he even walked along the very top of the garden wall, right up in the sky!"

But Humpy did not want to wait, and that night, when the rest of the family were asleep, he crawled away from the safe cabbage leaf and out into the world.

The first thing he came across was a forest made of thick, red trees with leaves even bigger than his cabbage leaf. He spent hours and hours creeping round and round these red trunks, and in and out, and when the sun rose he found himself on a wide, gritty path. It was black and very rough and hurt his tender body, and seemed to go on for ever. He only kept going because there was nowhere else to go.

When the path came to an end he found himself among great rocks with flowers and ferns growing over them. He liked this better as the rocks were wet with dew and the ferns gave patches of cool shade. Suddenly he stopped, and listened, and watched.

A great, big, creature with long legs and a sharp beak and speckled feathers was holding something and bashing it again and again against a stone. The thing was strangely familiar. Was it – could it be – a snail shell? The more he watched the more certain he became. Yes, it was a real snail shell and all around were more bits of broken shell that had once been live snails. But now they were alive no longer.

Humpy felt sick with fear and he only had one idea in his head, to get home to his mother as quickly as he could. He didn't know which way to turn, but he noticed a little, silvery track along the ground.

I'll follow that, he thought. It may lead me away from this horrible place.

He followed the silvery track for the rest of the day. It led him over the great rocks where the ferns grew, and along the gritty path and through the forest of red tree trunks, and just as the moon rose he found himself under the green cabbage leaf which was his home.

His mother listened to the story of his adventures and then, at the end, she said very seriously, "You are a lucky, little snail. The red forest was the rhubarb bed. The gritty road was a cinder path. The ferny rocks were the rockery. And the monster smashing snails on a stone was a hungry thrush. You might easily have been eaten up too. You would have been a tender morsel for him."

"And what was the silvery trail that led me home to you?" asked Humpy.

"Oh, that was the track all proper snails leave behind them, so they can find their way home and need never be lost."

My Scarecrow Grandad

Anne English

My funny Grandad pulled a horrible face. He waved his arms round and round like a windmill. "Get off!" he shouted. "Shoo!" The birds flew away as far as the fence and sat in a row, looking at Grandad and me.

It was the summer holidays, and I was helping Grandad on his allotment. He likes me helping him. He says I'm good company. We'd just finished planting two rows of tiny cabbage plants, and the birds were flying down to peck them. *And* they were eating the carrots and peas we'd planted earlier.

Grandad sat down on the upturned wooden box he used as a seat. His face was red, and he was puffing.

"Wretched birds," he grumbled, "they think the cabbage plants are for their dinner."

I said that I liked the birds.

"So do I," said Grandad, "but *not* on my allotment. I grow vegetables for us to eat, not for them. I grow them for Gran and me, and for you and your Mum and Dad, and for Uncle Ted and Aunt Elsie and Dave and Doreen. That's nine of us. And gardening's hard work, you know that."

The birds came back, squawking, and started digging in the soil with their beaks. Grandad pulled another horrible face, screwing up his eyes and twisting his mouth to one side. He shouted at them again, and nearly choked himself.

That's when we decided to make a scarecrow.

There's a shed on Grandad's allotment. He keeps his garden tools in it, a spade, a hoe, a rake, a trowel and a dibber, and lots of other things like sticks and string. He never throws anything out. The shed is so full that only one of us can get in at a time. But I don't mind staying outside – there's lots of dead flies in there.

We propped open the door with a big stone, and Grandad rummaged about inside the shed. I could hear thumps and bumps as he looked for things to make the scarecrow. Then he called to me.

"Put these on the path," he said, "and get ready to help me. It'll take two of us to make a scarecrow before tea time."

First he gave me the long wooden handle from a broom. Then he threw out an old red ball with a split in it. I used to play with that ball when I was smaller and couldn't help Grandad so much. Then he handed me an old smock pinafore of Gran's, with holes in the elbows and a torn pocket. I had to shake dust and spiders off it. Then he gave me a funny straw hat and a jar full of milk bottle tops. That made quite a pile on the path.

Grandad came out of the shed covered in dust. He was carrying a tin of green paint and a stick. He put them carefully on the ground.

"Right," he said. "Let's get the scarecrow's face done first. We must make it fierce, to frighten away the birds."

He sat on the wooden box and held the red ball on his knee.

"This can be the scarecrow's head. You take the green paint, and the stick for a paintbrush, and paint a face on it. Only remember, it has to be a horrible face, like this."

And he pulled his horrible, screwed-up, chasing-away-the-birds face.

I knelt in front of him, and dipped the stick in the paint. Then I looked at Grandad's face and started painting the ball.

I painted two cross-looking green eyes, and two scribbly eyebrows. Then I did a squashy nose and a raggy moustache.

"Hurry up," said Grandad, "or I might stick like this."

Quickly I made a big twisty mouth. The paint dripped down the ball, and the mouth looked as if it was full of pointed teeth.

I showed it to Grandad. "Horrible," he said, "just like my face."

Then he smiled, and he didn't look horrible at all.

We fixed the ball on top of the broom handle, and dressed the scarecrow in Gran's old pinafore and the funny straw hat. Then I had a clever idea. We threaded milk bottle tops on black thread and made long streamers. I fastened one round the scarecrow like a necklace, and we tied lots and lots round his hat. They blew in the wind and rattled – like a skeleton rattling his bones, Grandad said.

We both thought the best place to put the scarecrow was right in the middle of the vegetable patch. Grandad made a deep hole in the soil with the dibber. Then I tiptoed across to it, not stepping on any of the plants, and held the scarecrow upright in the hole, until Grandad had fixed it firmly.

There it stood, with its fierce red and green face, the clothes flapping and the milk bottle tops rattling.

"That should do the trick," said Grandad.

And it did. It frightened away all the birds, and all the cats, and nearly all the dogs. And ours was the only allotment with a scarecrow grandad.

August Weather

Dead heat and windless air,
  And silence over all;
Never a leaf astir,
  But the ripe apples fall;
Plums are purple-red,
  Pears amber and brown;
Thud! in the garden-bed!
  Ripe apples fall down.

Air like a cider-press
  With the bruised apples' scent;
Low whistles express
  Some sleepy bird's content;
Still world and windless sky,
  A mist of heat o'er all;
Peace like a lullaby,
  And the ripe apples fall.

Katharine Tynan

The Day it Rained Cats and Dogs

Linda Allen

It was a curious thing about Mrs Jenkins, but every once in a while her words had a strange way of coming true.

"Oh, blow!" she said to Mr Jenkins one day after she had stumbled over something in the road. Immediately the wind began to blow so hard that they had to cling to a tree until it had stopped.

"My dear," said Mr Jenkins, straightening his clothes, "you really will have to be careful what you say when these moods come over you. Let's go home and I will make you a nice cup of tea."

As Mrs Jenkins sipped her tea. Mr Jenkins said, "You just sit there quietly. I'll do the housework for you today."

"Thank you," said Mrs Jenkins gratefully. "I'll do as you say, although it does seem a shame to leave all that work to you. The kitchen is quite full of dirty pots and pans."

No sooner had she spoken than they heard a great clatter in the kitchen, and when Mr Jenkins opened the door he found that he could scarcely get into the room for all the pots and pans. They were piled up on the table and on the shelves, in the sink and on the chairs, from the floor right up to the ceiling. It was late in the evening by the time poor Mr Jenkins had finished washing them all.

The next day Mrs Jenkins was her usual self, and as the weeks went by she quite forgot to be careful about what she said. Then one morning, after she had done her washing and hung it outside to dry, she began to feel rather peculiar again. She didn't like to mention it to Mr Jenkins. I'll just sit down quietly, she thought, perhaps it will pass off.

She was just about to go into the sitting room when she happened to glance out of the window. "Oh!" she shouted angrily. "Look at that! My washing was almost ready to be ironed, and now look what's happening. It's raining cats and dogs!"

Immediately the black clouds parted, and out of the sky there came an absolute downpour of cats and dogs. Big dogs and little dogs, and nice cats and nasty cats, dozens of them falling everywhere, barking and meowing and fighting among themselves as they landed. Some of them splashed into the goldfish pool, and others twanged up and down on the clothes line. They ran up the trees and along the fences. They sat on the window sill and stared in at Mr and Mrs Jenkins.

"It's that Mrs Jenkins again!" cried the neighbours. "She's had one of her turns again. Why can't she be more careful when she feels them coming on? Shoo! Shoo! Go away!"

"It's only a shower," called out Mr Jenkins from an upstairs window. "It will be over in a minute or two."

But it wasn't. All the rest of the morning it rained cats and dogs around the Jenkins's house until there wasn't a patch of ground or an inch of fence that wasn't being sat upon.

"You've done it this time," said Mr Jenkins, shaking his head. "You've really done it. Pots and pans were bad enough, but at least we were able to give them away to our friends. Who on earth would want so many damp cats and dogs?"

Just after midday a policeman came to the door. "Are you the owner of these animals?" he asked Mr Jenkins. 'We've had a complaint."

"I'm sorry," apologized Mr Jenkins. "You see, it's my wife. She's had one of her turns again."

"I can't help that," said the policeman. "Just you keep these animals under control or we shall have to take action."

"Oh dear!" wailed Mrs Jenkins when he had gone. 'What can I do? I shall be seeing pink elephants next!"

There were two great thumps, and when Mr and Mrs Jenkins looked out of the kitchen window, they saw two pink elephants sitting on the lawn, looking rather dazed. The cats began to spit, and the dogs put their tails between their legs and howled. For a moment the elephants just looked at them; and then suddenly they trumpeted loudly and began to chase the cats and dogs.

Round and round the garden they went, out of the gate, and up the road, and the last that Mr and Mrs Jenkins saw of them they were disappearing over the hill.

Mrs Jenkins went out into the garden and brought in her washing. "I hope I never see anything like that again in the whole of my life," she said. Which was a good thing to say, because she never did, and from that day to this she hasn't had another turn.

Not yet, anyway.

The Angry Giant

Jean Watson

"I am outrageously, stupendously angry," roared Giant Colossal, one day.

"But why?" asked the earth-people.

"Shan't tell you," sulked the giant. "You will have to find that out for yourselves. And until you do, I shall sleep all day and stamp about all night."

"Oh, no, please don't!" begged the earth-people. But it was no use. The giant kept his word. He slept all day and stamped about all night, making the mountains rock and the waves roar. The earth-people couldn't get any sleep.

"We will have to find out why the giant is angry," they yawned.

"I know why the giant is angry," said the smallest girl in the world.

"Do be quiet!" said her elders, not really listening. Instead, they sent a world-famous dentist to see the giant. It took him a long time to wake up Giant Colossal.

"Er – have you got toothache, Giant?" asked the dentist nervously, "because I'd be very happy to take out the offending teeth."

The giant let out such a bellow that the little dentist shot straight out of his skin.

"No, I have not got toothache," roared Colossal, and the dentist slipped back into his skin and bolted. He told the earth-people that the giant's anger had nothing whatever to do with his teeth.

"I know why the giant is angry," said the smallest girl in the world.

"Oh, do be quiet!" said her elders, not really listening. Instead, they sent a world-famous shoe-maker to see the giant, who didn't look pleased to be woken up again.

"Excuse me, Mr Colossal," said the shoemaker. "Are your shoes tight, by any chance? A pinching shoe can be nasty, very nasty. You can't be too careful about shoes and I'd be only too pleased to fit you with a more suitable . . ."

But before he could finish, the giant snortled so loudly that the shoemaker dropped his bag of tools. They landed on the giant's big

82

toe. Colossal grasped his foot in his hands and hopped about, shrieking with pain.

"I'll give you pinching shoes, you clumsy shrimp!" he bellowed. The shoemaker scuttled away. He told the earth-people that the giant's anger had nothing whatever to do with his shoes.

"I know why the giant is angry," said the smallest girl in the world.

"Oh, do be quiet," said her elders, not really listening. Instead, they sent a world-famous doctor to see the giant. He was very tired after a long, hard night's stamping about.

"Are you ill, my dear fellow?" the doctor shouted, shaking the sleeping giant. "Allow me to examine you. If you sit up and stick out your tongue . . ."

But before he could finish, the giant started to grind his teeth, making a sound like falling rocks. The doctor tut-tutted and backed away. The giant then said, through clenched teeth, "No, I am not ill, but you will be if you don't get out of my bedroom this instant!"

The doctor walked away with as much dignity as his shaking knees would allow. He told the earth-people that the giant's anger had nothing to do with his health.

"I know why the giant is angry," said the smallest girl in the world.

"Oh, do be quiet," said her elders, not really listening to her. Instead, they sent a world-famous tailor to see the giant.

When he had managed to rouse Colossal, the tailor said, "Look, Sir Giant, I have designed a whole new suit of clothes for you."

He put some drawings on the bedside table, but the giant thumped this so hard with his fist that the papers and the tailor shot into the air.

"There is nothing whatever the matter with my clothes," he roared. The tailor came down to earth and skipped lightly out of the giant's reach, without even bothering to collect up his drawings. He told the earth-people that the giant's anger had nothing whatever to do with his clothes.

By this time the earth-people, having had no sleep for a week, were very tired indeed.

"We *must* find out why the giant is angry," they said.

"But I *know* why the giant is angry," said the smallest girl in the world in her loudest voice.

"What did you say?" asked her elders, listening to her properly for the first time.

"I said I know why the giant is angry."

"Then why didn't you tell us!" demanded the people.

"I've been trying to," said the smallest girl in the world, "but you keep telling me to be quiet. The giant is angry *because we forgot his birthday!*"

"So we did," exclaimed her elders. "His three hundredth birthday, too. No wonder he was annoyed!"

So they asked a world-famous cook to make a birthday cake as big as a pond and they took it to the giant, with the the smallest girl in the world leading the procession.

"Excuse me, Giant Colossal," said the smallest girl in the world. "But if you would allow me to, I will light your three hundred candles."

The giant opened his eyes. He saw the cake and all the people. Slowly a smile spread across his face.

"You remembered," he said, happily. "Late, but at least you remembered."

Then the smallest girl in the world climbed on to the cake, having taken her shoes and socks off, of course, and lit the three hundred candles. It took a long, long time.

Then everyone sang, "Happy birthday".

By this time the Giant was his usual jolly self again, so they all had a wonderful birthday party, and afterwards everyone had a good, quiet night's sleep!

September

George and the Mushrooms

Gwen Grant

George lived in a house in the middle of a field. There was a garden full of flowers and vegetables, stables for one horse and two ponies, a chicken house for the hens and chickens, a barn for Buttercup the cow, three goats, six pigs in a pig sty and two kennels for the black and white sheep dogs.

In the fields around the house were a flock of sheep and eight white geese.

One morning, George's father said, "All the fences and gates need mending with new pieces of wood," and he asked George if he would like to go with him to the wood-yard.

"Oh yes!" George said. "I like the wood-yard," so his father got out the old lorry from the barn and they drove to the wood-yard.

"Fill it up," George's father said to the woodman, and the woodman got in his rusty brown crane, carefully lifted the long pieces of wood, and dropped them into the back of the lorry.

When the lorry could hold no more, George's father paid the woodman and they returned home.

Before they had gone very far, the back of the lorry dropped open. George and his father didn't hear a thing. They didn't hear the first piece of wood fall off the back of the lorry on to the road – clunk! They didn't hear the other pieces of wood as they rolled out of the lorry too – clunk! clunk! clunk! Soon, the lorry was almost empty.

By the time Tom the roadsweeper came round the corner of the road with his brush and barrow, the lorry had gone.

"Why, whatever is this?" Tom said, staring at the long line of wood lying right down the edge of the road. "Am I supposed to sweep it all up? It will never go into my barrow," and he looked first at his little barrow and then at the long bits of wood.

"I don't think I'm supposed to sweep all that up," Tom said, brushing up a sleepy butterfly. The butterfly flew away.

Tom stared at the wood for a long time. "Why!" he said at last. "I know what it is. Someone's going to build a fence around the mushroom field," and he trundled the old barrow up the road, leaving all the wood exactly where it was.

85

The first person Tom met when he got into the village was Fred, the bell-ringer.

"Hello, Fred," Tom said. "Did you know someone is going to build a fence around the mushroom field?"

"What?" shouted Fred. "Build a fence around the mushroom field! That's awful! Where will we get our mushrooms from then?" and Fred raced away to ring the bells in the church.

"We shall have to put a stop to this," he said.

Soon the church bells were ringing out all over the village. Everyone stopped to listen. The fishmonger stopped his van. The tinker stopped his horse and cart and the cobbler stopped hammering nails into shoes.

In the fire station, the chief fireman was having a little sleep in his chair. The bells woke him and he jumped up and the chair fell over.

"My goodness!" the chief cried. "There's a fire somewhere. Fire! Fire!" he shouted and slid down the firemen's pole.

All the firemen rushed into the fire station and put on their shining helmets, tucked their axes into their belts, pulled on their big boots and jumped on to the fire-engine.

"Ring the bell! Ring the bell!" the chief roared.

Down the road they raced. "Jangle, jangle, jangle," went the bell.

By the time the fire-engine reached the church, everybody was standing around Fred the bell-ringer.

"Where's the fire? Where's the fire?" shouted the chief.

"Fire?" Tom the roadsweeper said. "There isn't any fire," and he told the chief about the fence which was going to be built around the mushroom field.

"Disgraceful!" roared the chief.

"Terrible!" shouted the fire brigade.

Fred the bell-ringer had painted some posters for everyone to carry, big white posters on long brown sticks.

"Hands off our mushrooms!" one poster said.

"No fences here!" said another.

"Go away!" said a third.

All the people in the village marched towards the mushroom field, their posters blowing in the wind, the chief, the fire-engine and the fire-brigade leading the way.

George and his father stopped their lorry near the house in the field.

"There's the church bells ringing," George said. "I wonder what's wrong?"

He looked down the road at a little cloud of dust.

"What's that?" he said pointing.

"People," George's father replied. "Lots of people."

Soon the people from the village were standing at the gate to the house in the field.

"Have you heard?" said Fred the bell-ringer. "Someone is going to build a fence around the mushroom field."

"How do you know?" George asked him.

"Tom the roadsweeper told me," Fred the bell-ringer replied.

"And how do *you* know?" George asked Tom the roadsweeper.

"Because there's a long line of wood all the way down the side of the field," Tom the roadsweeper said. "That's how I know."

George's father went round to the back of the lorry.

"There's no wood in the lorry," he said.

George and all the people from the village went to look at the empty lorry.

"It was full to the top," George told them all.

"It must have fallen out," Fred the bell-ringer said.

There was a long silence.

"What kind of wood is it?" asked the chief of the fire brigade, and George told him it was long wood.

"We're going to put new pieces of wood in the fences and the gates," he said.

"I think I know where your wood is," the chief cried. "Follow me!" and George, George's father, and all the people of the village followed the chief, his fire-brigade and the fire-engine.

When they got to the road outside the mushroom field, the chief said, "There you are! There's your wood."

George and his father said, "It's going to be a lot of work picking up all that wood and putting it back in the lorry."

"Do you mean it isn't a fence?" asked Fred the bell-ringer.

"No," George said. "It isn't a fence at all."

Fred the bell-ringer turned to Tom the roadsweeper.

"Now then," he said. "It isn't a fence at all."

"Thought it was," Tom the roadsweeper said quietly.

"Our mushrooms are safe now," the chief said and everyone cheered. Everyone except George and his father.

"We've got to pick up all that wood," they said.

"Well," said the chief. "As there isn't a fire, we'll help you."

So the chief, the fire-brigade, Tom the roadsweeper, Fred the bell-ringer and everyone in the village helped George and his father to pick up all their wood and put it back in the lorry.

"This time," George said. "I shall fasten the back of the lorry very carefully." And he did.

And this time they got all the wood safely back home.

"If I were an apple"

If I were an apple
And grew upon a tree,
I think I'd fall down
On a nice boy like me.
I wouldn't stay there
Giving nobody joy;
I'd fall down at once
And say, "Eat me, my boy."

Anon

Lazy Jack

A traditional tale

Once a poor old woman lived in a little cottage in the country. She had one son called Jack, who was very lazy. He would do nothing to help his mother; he was so lazy that all he did in summer was lie in the sun, and in winter he spent his time sitting by the fire. Finally, his mother became very angry and said, "Jack, I will turn you right out of this cottage unless you wake yourself up and go and do some work."

When Jack heard this he began to worry, and decided he had better try to find some work to do.

The next day he went off to a farmer, and agreed to work the whole day for him for one penny. At the end of the day, Jack proudly brought his penny away but, as he had never had any money before, he didn't know what to do with it. He tossed it up and down from one hand to the other until, finally, he lost it as he was crossing a little stream near his cottage. When his mother heard his story she was very cross and said, "You silly boy; you should have put it in your pocket."

"Oh, I'll remember next time, Mother," promised Jack.

The following day, Jack went to work for a cowman, who gave him a jar of milk for his day's work. Jack took the jar and put it into the large pocket of his jacket. Of course, all the milk was spilt long before he reached home!

"How silly you are," said his mother. "You should have carried it very carefully on your head."

"I'll do so next time, Mother," replied Jack.

The next day, Jack went to work for another farmer, who gave him a cream cheese to take home. Jack took the cheese and placed it very carefully on the top of his head. But, of course, by the time he arrived home the cheese had all melted! Some of it lay on the path and the rest was stuck to his hair. How funny he looked! His mother was again very cross and said, "You stupid boy! You should have carried it carefully in your hands."

"I'll do that next time, Mother," promised Jack.

The day afterwards, Jack found work with a baker, and in the evening the baker gave him a large tom-cat. Jack took hold of the cat and placed it carefully in his hands. In a short time the cat began to scratch and, in the end, it scratched him so much that he had to let it go. When he got home and told his mother, she said to him, "What a silly fellow you are. You should have tied a string to it and dragged it along after you."

"Oh, I'll certainly do that next time, Mother," answered Jack.

The following day, which was Saturday, Jack went to work for a butcher. In the evening the butcher gave him a fine shoulder of mutton for their Sunday dinner. Jack was very pleased. He tied a piece of string to the mutton and pulled it along the ground behind him, all along the roads and pathways. Of course, by the time he got home the meat was completely spoilt.

"You stupid good-for-nothing," scolded his mother. "Now we have only cabbage for our Sunday dinner. You should have carried the meat on your shoulder."

"I'll do that next time, Mother," promised Jack.

On Monday, Jack went to work for the cowman again, and this time he was given a donkey to take home. After a long struggle, he managed to hoist the donkey on to his shoulders, and then he started to stagger down the road with it as best he could.

Now, on his way home, he had to go past the house of a rich man and his daughter. The daughter was very beautiful, but everyone was very sad because she was also deaf and dumb. She had never laughed once in all her life, and the doctors said that she would never be able to speak until someone made her laugh. Many people had come from far and wide to try to make her laugh. They had danced comic dances, told funny stories, sung funny songs, but she had never laughed once. Finally, her father had promised that the first man who made her laugh would be able to marry her and share his fortune.

That evening the girl was staring sadly out of the window, when a most peculiar sight came into view. It was a young man carrying a real live donkey on his shoulders! How strange and comical he looked! As soon as the young girl saw him she burst out laughing, and she laughed and laughed until the tears rolled down her cheeks. When her father heard her laughing he was so happy that he ran out at once and called Jack in. He kept the promise he had made and, a short while after, a great feast was held and Jack was married to his beautiful bride. They went to live in a fine house, and invited Jack's mother to live with them; and there they all lived happily together for the rest of their lives.

Hullo, Jacko!

Eileen Colwell

Jacko was a monkey puppet, with twinkling black eyes, a round head with two neat ears and a wide mouth which was always smiling. His body was made of red towelling and he had a long red tail.

Jacko belonged to a lady called Miss Hallam who went about telling stories to children. He liked to hear the children shout "Hullo, Jacko!" when Miss Hallam took him out of her bag. Then he would smile all over his face and wave his hands at them.

Jacko travelled everywhere with Miss Hallam and it was on one of these journeys that a dreadful thing happened. Miss Hallam had taken him out of her bag to cheer up a little boy who was crying on the opposite seat of the carriage. He stopped crying at once when Jacko stroked his hand gently and smiled.

The train was hot and Miss Hallam dozed off. She only woke up when the train stopped at her station. Startled, she picked up her bag and jumped out onto the platform. The little boy and his mother got off as well. But Jacko had slipped off the seat and was left behind.

It was very dirty under the seat and Jacko didn't like the sticky toffee papers there, so he went to sleep. He usually slept when Miss Hallam didn't need him.

The train ran on for many miles and finally stopped for the night at a big London station. As the guard walked along the carriages to check that the windows were shut, he noticed something red under a seat. It was Jacko!

"Hullo!" said the guard. "Who's left you behind? I'll have to take you to the Lost Property Office in the morning, but tonight I'll take you home."

So he did, and his little boy, who was only two, loved Jacko and took him to bed with him. All night Jacko lay at his side and dreamed of Miss Hallam.

In the morning, the guard put Jacko in a bag and took him to the Lost Property Office. "I'm sure your owner will find you," he said consolingly. "Keep smiling!"

The clerk pinned a number on to his coat and put him on a shelf. What a strange place he was in! He could see umbrellas, bags, gloves, ladies' hats, odd shoes, lumpy parcels with the paper coming off, a bicycle and a kite.

A Teddy Bear was sitting next to him. "Have you been here long?" asked Jacko.

"Far too long," said the Teddy. "The little girl who lives with me must have missed me dreadfully."

"Are we ever found?" asked Jacko anxiously.

"Sometimes, I think," said Teddy Bear. "Things disappear and I never see them again."

At first a cuckoo clock struck every hour and a bird popped out and said, "Cuckoo," several times. But after two days the clock ran down and the friendly bird was silent.

The days went by and Jacko grew very sad. Where was Miss Hallam? He missed the children who had called, "Hullo, Jacko!" His friend, Teddy Bear, tried to cheer him up but he drooped a little more each day.

One day, however, several men came in carrying a lot of mysterious packages.

"What are those men going to do?" asked Jacko.

"I don't know," said Teddy, "but those things they are carrying are cameras."

The men clattered about, looking on all the shelves. "What a lot of old junk!" said one of them. "Why here's a cuckoo clock."

"And look at this hat!" said another, putting on a large hat with feathers.

"I can't understand why people forget such things," said the first man. "How can they leave *one* shoe or a handbag or a brief case?"

"Or their spectacles – or their teeth!" exclaimed another.

The men were from a television company and they were making a film about the work of the Lost Property Office and the odd things people leave behind on trains and buses.

They set up their cameras and began to film what was on the shelves. "Some kiddy will be sad to have lost this teddy bear," said one. "Perhaps he'll see it on the film . . ."

"Here's something that's fun," said a man they called Bill. He picked up Jacko and put his hand inside his glove body. Jacko felt much better at once, much more alive.

"My boy has a puppet that works like this," said Bill, moving his fingers. "Come on now, wave! A lot of people will be watching you, you know."

Jacko didn't know but he waved his hand and smiled and smiled. Presently the men finished their filming and went away. It seemed very quiet and lonely when they had gone.

Miss Hallam had been very sad to lose Jacko. For a whole week she had made enquiries but without success.

That afternoon she had sat down for a rest. The television was on and she glanced at it now and then to see if there was anything interesting.

"What odd things people leave behind them when they travel," came the voice of the presenter. "Let me show you a few items which are in the Lost Property Office at this very moment."

Miss Hallam watched without much interest. The camera moved along the shelves – a cuckoo clock, a plant in a pot, a lady's hat, a wheelbarrow, a wig, a teddy bear, and then a small glove puppet with a neat round head, black eyes, a long tail and a mouth with rather an anxious smile. The puppet was waving.

"JACKO!" exclaimed Miss Hallam. "So that's where you are!"

She rang up the Lost Property Office at once. "Yes," said the clerk, a puppet like the one she described had been handed in. If she would call and prove it was hers, she could claim it any time.

The very next morning, Jacko saw Miss Hallam walk into the office. He couldn't wave his hand but he smiled and smiled so that she would be sure to see him.

And she did! "Hullo, Jacko!" she said, and they both went home together happily.

The Loaf Cottage

Muriel Pearson

Something had gone wrong with the cooker in Class Ten, or
something had gone wrong with the bread that the children were
baking. The loaf had become too large for the oven and it was
getting bigger all the time. With a large thud the loaf landed on the
floor and continued to grow.

"We've put too much yeast into it," called Katie. "Who measured the yeast today?"

But it didn't really matter who had measured the yeast for the
children had an enormous loaf of bread on the classroom floor, and
it was still rising.

"Push it out into the corridor," called somebody. So they just
managed to squeeze the swelling loaf into the wide corridor. There
it continued to grow and grow.

"Push it out into the playground," called another voice.

The children heaved and pushed. The loaf rolled through the
swing doors and out into the playground. There it lay, still getting
bigger.

The loaf of bread was now so huge that the children could no
longer move it. They watched in amazement as the loaf grew larger
and larger, until it was the size of a cottage. And then it suddenly
stopped growing. There it sat, in the middle of the playground, a
gigantic loaf with a brown, crusty top, looking like a house without
a door or any windows.

"Let's make a door," said Jonathan. The children began to cut
slices out of the side of the loaf and very soon they had made rather
a lop-sided entrance. And, of course, they had to eat the bread
they had removed. It was still warm and fresh and tasted wonderful.

They were so pleased with what they had done that they started
to make some windows. Before long, they had four, rather crooked
windows, two at the front and two at the back. They spread the
slices of bread with jam and they ate them up. The bread was still
lovely and fresh though not quite as warm as before.

This was the most exciting project that Class Ten had ever done.

Instead of doing lessons for the next few days, they spent their time removing hundreds of slices of bread from the inside of the loaf. They ate bread and jam for breakfast, bread and butter for dinner and bread and honey for tea.

Each day the bread grew a little harder and by the end of the week it was nearly as hard as toast. But this was a good thing because the loaf was now hollow and its four walls were firm and strong and able to hold the crusty brown roof safely on top.

"I'm glad that's finished," groaned Philip. "I don't want to eat any more bread for a very long time."

All the children agreed that they had eaten too much. But they were very proud of their loaf cottage.

On Friday their teacher brought four very large turnips into the classroom.

"It's Hallowe'en tomorrow," she said. "We're going to make turnip lanterns to frighten the witches away."

The children in Class Ten were soon busy removing the insides of the turnips. Having already removed the inside of a gigantic loaf, they found that tackling the turnips was very easy.

By the end of the afternoon they had made four beautiful turnip lanterns. The children had cut slits in the sides of the turnips so that they looked like eyes and grinning mouths. Each contained a little candle.

"These should frighten the witches away," said their teacher.

"Where shall we hang them?" asked Jonathan, but everyone had the same idea, "Hang them in the windows of the loaf cottage and then we can have a Hallowe'en party in there tomorrow."

On Saturday evening the air was crisp and cold. The night was dry and still and very, very dark. It was just the kind of night that witches enjoy. The loaf cottage in the playground was beautifully lit with the turnip lanterns. They flickered and cast trembling shadows on the playground.

It was the best party the children had ever been to. They were relieved that there were no sandwiches as they had had more than enough bread that week. Instead, they ate biscuits shaped like witches, chocolate broomsticks and gingerbread cats. They pretended that the lemonade was magic and that it turned them into hooting owls, flapping ghosts, cackling witches and stealthy cats. They had a wonderful time and made a lot of noise. They pretended to cast spells on each other, turning into princes and princesses, frogs, kangaroos, dancing bears and tumbling clowns.

95

They had great fun and their laughter spilled out into the dark playground.

When they left the cottage to go home, the night seemed eerie and unfriendly. All the birds except the owls were asleep. The moon peeped out from behind the clouds. The children stole home to bed, looking round carefully to make sure that there were no witches about. They had just reached their homes when the first big raindrops began to fall. The moon disappeared behind heavy clouds and the rain began to splash on to the playground.

The flickering turnip lanterns were soon full of rain-water and the lights sizzled and went out. The brown crusty roof became very damp and soft. The firm walls of the loaf cottage sagged as they too became soft and wet. The loaf cottage was collapsing. With a long sigh it fell at last into a heap of soft wet dough. During the night it was gradually washed away so that when the children returned to school on Monday morning there was no sign of the loaf cottage. Nobody would even have guessed that anything unusual had taken place.

Autumn

The rustle of leaves,
A chill in the air,
The crackling of bonfires,
The shouts of a child;
The scent of the corn in newly ploughed fields,
The smell of damp earth;
The sparkling of dew in the hazy sunshine,
The stormy wind blowing:
These are the signs that Autumn is here.

An eleven year old

The Kitten who Hated the Dark

Ruth Hoult

Montgomery, the kitten, peeped under the stable door.

"It's dark outside," he said. "I'm not going out. Dark is horrible and nasty. It's not nice at all."

Peter, the pony, who lived in the stable, too, looked at Montgomery over the top of his stall.

"Stuff and nonsense," he said. "All kittens like the dark. They always go out at night."

"Not this one," replied Montgomery, shaking his little black head. "Have you any idea what I can do about it, please? The dark is horrid."

"Wait for the moon to come out," suggested Peter. "Then it will not be dark any more."

When the moon rose in the sky lighting up the stable yard, Montgomery went out to play.

But not for long.

With an oooooooooh, oooooooooh, oooooooooh, the wind came; blowing dark clouds across the sky and hiding the silver moon. Everything was very dark and Montgomery sat down miaowing loudly for the clouds to go away, but they didn't. The night stayed as dark as dark as could be.

Montgomery returned to the brightly lit stable. He sat, a gloomy looking little ball of fur, on top of Peter's stall.

"The moon has gone behind the clouds," he said unhappily. "And I've just remembered the moon doesn't shine every night. Please, what am I to do?"

"Well," replied Peter. "You will have to go out when it is day-time."

"I can't do that," exclaimed Montgomery. "I sleep during the day."

"Then," said Peter firmly. "There is only one thing you can do. You must find a lighthouse; they shine all night long. I don't know what they look like. It's only what I've heard. But I'm sure you will find one, if you search hard enough."

The very next time there was a moon, Montgomery set out to look for a lighthouse.

He came to a place where there was a lot of light, and saw a funny funnel with flames coming out of the top.

There was also a cat; a grey fluffy cat, rubbing itself along a fence.

"Please, is this a lighthouse?" Montgomery asked him.

The cat stopped its rubbing and shook its head.

"This is an oil refinery," it said, looking very superior. "It isn't at all like a lighthouse. The light is not as bright."

Montgomery was disappointed. He thanked the cat, then set off once more to find a lighthouse.

It wasn't long before he came to a large building with light streaming from its window. There were lots of people inside and out, and cars, vans and lorries parked all around.

In one of the cars Montgomery saw a Siamese cat. It was looking disdainfully out of the back window.

"Excuse me for bothering you, but is this a lighthouse?" asked Mongomery.

The Siamese cat looked down his nose. "This is a motorway service station," it replied. "It's not the least bit like a lighthouse. The light is not as bright."

Montgomery knew he must not give up. He thanked the Siamese cat and set off again.

He came to a place with long lines of lights; some green, some red, some yellow.

"Can this be a lighthouse?" he said to himself.

Then he saw a tall building with lights at the top. He went to investigate. Outside the door he found a large ginger cat preening itself.

"Please, can you tell me if this is a lighthouse?" asked Montgomery. "I have come such a long way to find one."

The cat stopped preening itself. "I'm sorry this is not a lighthouse," the cat replied. "This is an airport. The light here is not as bright. If you want to find a lighthouse, you must go to the sea."

"To the sea, thank you, I will," answered Montgomery.

Montgomery went to the sea.

The first thing he saw was a tall, round building standing on the rocks. It had a flashing light at the top that made everything as bright as if it were day.

Montgomery could see the thin line of the sea in the distance, the sand, the cliff, and a row of cottages along the cliff top.

Then he saw a large, tabby cat walking jauntily down the cliff path.

"Excuse me, please," said Montgomery, "But is that a light-house?"

"It is," answered the cat. "The best in England. I should know because I live there. I'm on shore leave at the moment."

"Then they won't want a kitten," said Montgomery sadly, telling the cat his problem.

"Don't look so glum," the cat said. "It would be just as light living in the cottages. I happen to know Mrs Pepper, at the end cottage, is looking for a kitten. Why not try to make friends with her?"

Montgomery thanked the tabby cat, then went to sit outside Mrs Pepper's cottage.

It wasn't long before Mrs Pepper opened her door to take in her bottle of milk.

"Miaow," said Montgomery promptly. And rubbed himself against her legs.

"My," said Mrs Pepper looking pleased. "I do want a kitten, but I didn't expect to find one on my door-step."

She opened the door wider. Montgomery walked in.

Mrs Pepper put down a large saucer of milk.

"I do hope you will stay," she said.

Montgomery did.

He washed himself, then purred and purred and purred.

"Light is pleasant. Light is happy, light is the nicest thing of all," said Montgomery to himself.

He curled up into a tiny ball, and went fast asleep. It was morning.

Mrs Simkin's Bathtub

Linda Allen

"Are you aware," said Mr Simkin to Mrs Simkin one morning, "that the bathtub's half-way down the stairs?"

"How very inconvenient," said Mrs Simkin, going to have a look, "How long has it been there?"

"I have no idea," said Mr Simkin. "It was in the bathroom when I went to bed last night, and now it's here, so it must have moved when we were asleep."

"Well, we shall just have to make the best of it," said Mrs Simkin. "Will you bath first, or shall I?"

"I will," said Mr Simkin bravely.

He stepped into the bathtub. It wobbled a bit at first, but it soon settled down. Mrs Simkin fetched soap and towels, shampoo and bath salts, and arranged them nicely on the stairs.

"There," she said, "it doesn't look too bad now, and if I polish the taps and scrub the feet it should look quite smart. I'm sure none of the neighbours has a bathtub on the stairs."

Mr Simkin said she was probably right.

After a day or two they hardly noticed that the bathtub was there at all. It didn't really inconvenience them to squeeze past it when they wanted to go upstairs, and the landing smelt so pleasantly of bath oil that Mrs Simkin began to feel quite happy about it.

She invited the lady next door to have a look, but the lady next door said that she didn't approve of these modern ideas, and anyhow, she had never been one to give herself airs.

One morning Mr Simkin went to have his bath. "My dear!" he cried. "Come and see! The bathtub's gone!"

"Gone!" cried Mrs Simkin, leaping out of bed. "Gone where?"

"I don't know," said Mr Simkin, "but it isn't on the stairs."

"Perhaps it's back in the bathroom," said Mrs Simkin.

They went to have a look, but it wasn't there.

"We shall have to buy another one," said Mr Simkin, as they went down to breakfast.

The bathtub was in the kitchen.

"You know, my dear," said Mr Simkin a few minutes later, "this is a much better place for a bathtub than half-way down the stairs. I quite like having breakfast in the bath."

"Yes," said Mrs Simkin, "I like it here, too. The bath towels match the saucepans, and think of all the soup I shall be able to make when we have a large dinner party."

"That's a very good point," agreed Mr Simkin. "I can't think why everybody doesn't want a bathtub in their kitchen."

One day Mr Simkin and Mrs Simkin went downstairs to find that the bathtub had moved again. It was in the living room, sitting snugly before the fire.

"Oh, I don't think I like it there," said Mrs Simkin, looking at it with her head on one side.

"Neither do I," said Mr Simkin, "although it will be very pleasant bathing in front of the fire."

"I don't suppose it will stay there very long," whispered Mrs Simkin. "Once a bathtub has started to roam it never knows when to stop."

She was quite right. The following morning the bathtub was underneath the sideboard, which was rather difficult for bathing, but they managed somehow. Two or three days later they found the bathtub in the basement with spiders in it.

On the day that Mrs Simkin was forty-two years old they couldn't find the bathtub anywhere.

"What shall I do?" cried Mrs Simkin. "I wanted to use that lovely bubble bath that you gave me for my birthday."

"So did I," said Mr Simkin.

The lady next door came round.

"Happy birthday," she said, "did you know that your bathtub was on the front lawn?"

They all went to have a look.

There was a horse drinking out of it.

"Go away," said Mrs Simkin to the horse. "How dare you drink my bath water, you greedy creature?" and she stepped recklessly into the bathtub.

The lady next door said she didn't know what the world was coming to and she went home and locked herself indoors.

As the bubbles floated down the street lots of people came to see what was going on. They saw Mrs Simkin sitting in the bathtub.

They were very interested.

They leaned on the fence and watched.

They asked if they could come again.

As the days went by Mrs Simkin began to think that the bathtub would stay on the front lawn for ever, but one morning when there was rather a chilly wind about they found the bathtub in the greenhouse.

The people in the street were very disappointed.

They got up a petition asking Mr Simkin to bring it back.

"My dear," said Mr Simkin a few days later, "do you happen to know where the bathtub is today?"

"No, Stanley," said Mrs Simkin, "but today's Tuesday. It's quite often in the garage on Tuesdays."

"It isn't there today," said Mr Simkin.

"Have you tried the verandah?" suggested Mrs Simkin. "It hasn't been there for some time."

"I've looked everywhere," said Mr Simkin. "It isn't in the house and it isn't in the garden."

Mrs Simkin was busy with something else.

"I do hope it hasn't gone next door," she sighed. "The lady next door has no sympathy with that kind of thing."

Mr Simkin went to enquire.

The lady next door said that she wouldn't allow anyone else's bathtub in her house, and that she was of the opinion that people ought to be able to control their bathtubs.

Mr Simkin went home.

Mr Robinson from across the street rang up.

"I know it's none of my business," he said, "but I thought you'd like to know that your bathtub's sitting up on the roof of your house."

Mrs Simkin thanked him for the information.

Mr Simkin went to take his bath. He said there was a marvellous view from up there.

Mrs Simkin climbed up. All the people cheered. She thought it was rather nice, but she had no head for heights. Perhaps it was time to ring up the plumber.

The plumber said that wandering bathtubs weren't really in his line of business and why didn't they get in touch with the Department of the Environment?

Mrs Simkin said that she wasn't going to all that trouble. She would soon get used to bathing on the roof.

So they left the bathtub where it was.

And that's where it liked to be best of all.

The people in the street had a meeting in Mr Simkin's green-house. They decided to have their bathtubs on their roofs as well.
All except the lady next door.
She preferred to take a shower.

A Leaf in the Shape of a Key

Joan Aiken

Leaves were falling from the trees, because it was the second day of November. It was also the day after Tim's birthday, and he had a new tricycle to ride in the garden.

First he fed the snails, who lived by the garden pool, with some orange jelly left over from his birthday tea. The snails loved orange jelly, and ate up a whole plateful. Tim would also have given some jelly to the stone goblin who sat by the garden pool, but the goblin was not fond of jelly. In fact he never ate anything at all. He always looked gloomy and bad-tempered. Perhaps this was because one of his feet was stuck underneath a large rock.

"Would you like a ride on my tricycle?" Tim suggested. The goblin's eyes flashed. He looked as if he would like a ride very much.

But that was no good either, because Tim couldn't lift the rock, which was very heavy indeed.

Tim went off, riding his tricycle over the grass. The stone goblin stared after him.

Leaves were fluttering down all over the lawn, and because there had been a frost the night before the grass was all crunchy with white frost crystal.

As Tim pedalled about, he began catching the leaves as they floated down near him, and putting them in the basket of his tricycle. He caught a red leaf, a yellow leaf, a brown leaf, a pale-green leaf, a dark-green leaf, and a silvery leaf. Then he caught another red leaf, two more brown leaves, and two more yellow leaves. Then he caught a great green leaf, the shape of a hand. Presently his basket was almost filled up with leaves. He pedalled back to the pool and showed all his leaves to the snails and the stone goblin.

"Look! I have caught twelve leaves!"

Now the goblin began to pay attention. "If you have caught twelve leaves, all different," he said, "that's magic."

Tim spread his leaves on the grass, and the goblin counted them.

"That one is a walnut leaf. And that's an oak leaf. This is a maple leaf. And that is from a silver birch. This one is from an apple tree.

104

And that is a copper-beech leaf. And here we have an ash-leaf. And you also have a cob-nut leaf, a pear-tree leaf, a rose leaf, a mulberry leaf and a fig-leaf. You are a very lucky boy, Tim. You have caught twelve leaves, and all of them are different."

"What must I do now?" said Tim, very excited.

"You must catch one more leaf. And that will give you what you want most in the whole world."

On his birthday yesterday Tim had been given his tricycle, and a lot of other presents and he felt already he had most of the things he wanted. But there *was* one thing.

"Oh!" he said. "What I would *really* like is to be able to get into the little cave up above the garden pool."

There was a steep bank on one side of the garden pool – almost like a little cliff – where water came trickling out of a hole and ran down into the pool. In the cliff there was a tiny cave. It was no bigger than the inside of a teapot. You could see into it, and it was very beautiful, all lined with moss like green velvet. There were tiny flowers growing in the moss, no bigger than pin-heads. They were blue and white. Tim longed to be small enough to get inside this beautiful place.

The stone goblin's eyes flashed again.

"Ride off on your tricycle," he said, "and catch one more leaf. Then bring it here. You must bring me the very first leaf that you catch."

Tim rode off at top speed. Almost at once a leaf came fluttering down in front of him and fell right into his basket.

"Watch out!" shouted a blackbird, swooping past him, very low. "Don't trust that goblin! He means mischief! I can see it in his eye."

But Tim took no notice of the blackbird's warning. He pedalled quickly back to the goblin with the thirteenth leaf in his basket.

"Here it is," he said, and took it out.

The thirteenth leaf was pale brown, and it was in the shape of a key.

"Look in the middle of my stomach," said the goblin, "and you'll find a keyhole." Tim looked, and he found the keyhole.

"Put in the key and unlock it," said the goblin.

Tim put the key into the hole and turned it. It was very stiff. But it did turn.

As soon as it had turned the goblin began to grow bigger. He pulled his foot out from under the heavy rock. He stood up, rather stiffly.

"That's better!" he said.

He was still growing, bigger and bigger.

"You promised that I should get into the cave," said Tim.

"So you shall," said the goblin.

He picked Tim up easily in his hand, reached over the pool, and put him into the cave.

"Why!" exclaimed Tim. "*You* weren't growing bigger! *I* was growing smaller!"

He was tremendously happy to be in the cave, and he began to clamber about, looking at the beautiful flowers. Now they seemed as big as teacups. But Tim found that, now he was so small, he sank up to his knees in the thick wet green moss, which was not very comfortable. Still, he was so pleased to be there that for some time he did not look out through the doorway, till he heard the blackbird squawking again.

When Tim looked out he had quite a shock. For the stone goblin had climbed on to his tricycle and was pedalling away.

"Well, I did offer him a ride before," thought Tim.

But then he saw that the goblin was pedalling towards the garden gate, which opened into the road.

"Stop, stop!" shouted Tim. "I'm not allowed to go out there! It's dangerous!"

But Tim had grown so small that his voice came out only as a tiny squeak. The goblin may not have heard. He took no notice at all. He was waving his arms about, singing and shouting, and pedalling crazily from side to side.

"I'm free!" he was shouting. "At last I'm free! I can go anywhere I want! I can go all over the world!"

Then Tim found out a frightening thing. He was so small that the little cliff under the cave entrance seemed terribly high to him and there was no way down it. He was stuck in the cave.

"Help!" he shouted to the goblin. "I can't climb down! Please come back and lift me."

"*I'm* not going to help you!" shouted the goblin. "You should have thought of that before. You'll just have to stay there! Goodbye! You'll never see me again!"

And he pedalled right out of the garden gate.

Poor Tim stared down the terribly steep cliff at the pool below. It looked like a huge lake. What ever shall I do? he wondered. Mum and Dad will never find me here. They'll never think of looking. I'm smaller than a mouse. I can't shout loud enough for them to hear. I shall have to stay in this cave for ever and ever. What shall I eat?

He sat down miserably on the wet green moss.

But he had not been sitting there very long when, to his surprise, he saw four long horns with eyes at their tips come poking up over the sill of the doorway. The horns belonged to two snails who had come climbing up the cliff. Snails don't mind how steep a cliff is, because they can stick themselves to the rock with their own glue.

"Don't worry now, Tim," they said kindly. "Just you hold on to us. We'll soon get you down the cliff. Hold tight on to our shells."

They turned themselves round. Tim put an arm tight round each of their shells, and they went slowly down the cliff, head-first. It was a bit frightening for Tim because they crawled so very slowly; he had rather too much time to look down. In the end he found it was better to look at the snails' shells, covered with beautiful pink and brown and yellow patterns, or to watch the clever way they stretched out their long necks and then pulled in their strong tails.

At last they came to the bottom of the cliff, and then, very carefully, they crawled round the stone edge of the pool, until Tim was safely back on the grass again, beside the empty plate, which seemed as big as a whole room.

"Oh, thank you!" he said. "I thought I would *never* get out of there. It was very kind of you!"

"It was nothing," said the snails politely. "After all, you gave us all that orange jelly."

Tim was safely out of the cave. But he was still tiny, much smaller than a mouse, and he didn't know what to do about that. And the stone goblin had gone off with his tricycle.

But just at that moment he heard a tremendous crash, somewhere outside in the road.

And at that very same moment, Tim grew back to his right size again.

Five minutes later Tim's father came into the garden, looking both angry and puzzled. He was carrying Tim's tricycle.

"Tim! How did this get into the road?" he said. "I found it up by the cross-roads. The wheel is bent – some car must have run into it. And there are bits of broken stone all over the street. Have you been riding out there? You know you're not allowed to do that!"

"The stone goblin took it," said Tim.

"Don't talk nonsense!"

"But look. He's gone!"

107

Tim's father looked at the empty place where the goblin had been, and at the heavy rock. It was much too heavy for Tim to have lifted.

Tim's father scratched his head. Then he fetched his tools and straightened out the bent wheel. "No riding in the street, now!" he said.

"Of course not," said Tim.

He began riding over the grass again. He caught lots more falling leaves. But he never again caught twelve different kinds.

The stone goblin never came back.

But whenever there was orange jelly for tea, Tim remembered to give some to the snails.

Fireworks

They rise like sudden fiery flowers
That burst upon the night,
Then fall to earth in burning showers
Of crimson, blue and white.

Like buds too wonderful to name,
Each miracle unfolds,
And catherine-wheels begin to flame
Like whirling marigolds.

Rockets and roman-candles make
An orchard of the sky,
When magic trees their petals shake
Upon each gazing eye.

James Reeves

Janik and the Magic Balls

Based on a story from Bohemia
Retold by Rhoda Power

Once upon a time there lived a poor gardener who worked for a rich farmer. His name was Janik, and his wife was called Ludmila.

Ludmila had a little white lamb called Baabaa. And *how* she loved it!

Janik often used to say, "Oh, Ludmila, whatever would you do without Baabaa!"

And Ludmila answered, "I'm sure I don't know, Janik! What would *you* do?"

Then, of course, they both laughed and said, "We couldn't possibly do without Baabaa."

But a day came when they had to do without their precious little lamb.

It happened like this. Janik was at work, picking up fallen apples in his master's garden, when suddenly the farmer burst into the orchard in a towering rage.

"Now then," he said, "what are you doing there? So that's it, is it? Stealing the apples."

Janik looked up in astonishment. "If you please, sir, I was picking them up for you."

The farmer snorted. "Huh! That's a likely story. I've missed several windfalls lately. I believe you've been feeding that wretched lamb of yours."

Janik began to get annoyed. "Lambs do not eat apples," said he.

"No, but their masters do!" said the farmer. "Here's your week's money. Now be off, and don't let me see you again!"

Janik trudged home very slowly. He knew that there was no one else with a garden, and he was afraid that he would never be able to get work. And, of course, no work meant no money. And no money meant no food.

When Ludmila heard what had happened she was very sad, and even Baabaa seemed less frisky than usual. For a week or two the poor woman eked out the money as well as she could. She and Janik ate very little and tramped about all over the country trying to find work. But it was of no use. Although it wasn't true, everyone seemed to think that Janik was a thief, and no one would have anything to do with him.

At last a day came when there was no money and no food in the house. All the furniture, Janik's Sunday coat, Baabaa's little silver bell and Ludmila's shawl were sold, and there was nothing left.

Ludmila began to cry. "It can't be helped," she said, "You – you – Oh dear! Oh dear! Y-you must s-s-sell Baabaa."

"Baabaa!" bleated a little voice, and Ludmila ran away so that she shouldn't hear it.

Poor Janik stooped down to stroke Baabaa. With a heavy heart he tied a piece of string round the little creature's neck and led it out of the cottage into the dusty road.

At that moment the world looked very black for Janik. He could hardly bear it. He tried to whistle to keep up his spirits, but he only choked, and at last he just trudged along with his shoulders hunched up and his chin on his chest. For many miles he walked, till he came to a gap in the hedge.

"Hallo! hallo!" cried a voice. "Are you going to market with that lamb?"

"Yes," said Janik gruffly, without looking round.

"Not so fast! Not so fast!" said the voice, and Janik felt a skinny hand grasp him by the wrist.

He looked down, and there was a little old woman no higher than a kitchen chair, and with cheeks as rosy as apples. She had a ball in her hand, and she kept throwing it up in the air as she spoke.

"You're in trouble, Janik," said she. "In trouble about some apples which you never stole in your life. Never mind, never mind. I'll take Baabaa and you shall have my ball."

"Ball," said Janik angrily. "What's the use of a ball to me? I want bread."

"Janik," said the old woman earnestly, "give me Baabaa and take my ball. You'll never regret it. Go home, shut the doors and windows, put the ball on the floor or the table, clap your hands and say,

'Ball, whenever my hands I clap
Remember your manners and raise your cap!'

If you do that, you'll be rich forever."

The old woman looked so serious, and Baabaa rubbed her head against Janik's knee as much as to say, "Master, dear, do as you're told," so Janik, at last, agreed to give his lamb in exchange for the ball.

He felt very doubtful about the exchange, and very sad when he said "Good-bye" to Baabaa; but still, a bargain's a bargain, and it was done now, so he couldn't grumble.

When he reached his cottage, he told Ludmila all about it. Together they went into the kitchen. Then Janik shut the door and the window, put the ball on the table, clapped his hands and said,

"Ball, whenever my hands I clap
Remember your manners and raise your cap!"

Before they had time to say anything more, the ball bounced off the table and broke in half. Out of each half jumped a little man in leather trousers and a green apron. Before Janik had recovered from his astonishment, they were running round the kitchen, laying the table with knives and forks and crockery and a delicious meal.

And I think you'll agree with me that this was really most extraordinary, because all the furniture had been sold, and there was no food in the house.

You can imagine how astonished Ludmila was too. Naturally, she had to try her luck.

"Ahem!" said she, very nervously, and clapped her hands,

"Ball, whenever my hands I clap,
Remember your manners and raise your cap!"

The ball opened, out bounced the two little men, and lo and behold, they had with them her own little white lamb, Baabaa, alive and kicking, just the same as ever, and frisking for joy!

Well, I suppose you can guess that, with a ball like that in the house, the gardener and his wife soon became very rich. Unfortunately, they were so delighted that they talked too much. The neighbours all came to see the magic ball, and at last the wicked farmer heard about it and came round to see, too.

"Good-day, Janik!" said he. "I know you don't feel very friendly towards me, but I dare say you'll show me your ball."

"Certainly, sir," said Janik, "here it is!"

He showed the ball. And what do you think that farmer did? He snatched the ball out of Janik's hand and put it in his own pocket, saying, "Thanks! I'll take that in exchange for the apples you stole."

And he walked out of the house, jumped on to his horse and galloped away. Of course, Janik went after him, but day after day the farmer grew richer, and day after day he refused to give back the ball.

At last Janik decided to go and look for the little old woman with the cheeks like apples. This time, he took a cow with him, and sure enough, when he came to a gap in the hedge out popped the little old woman.

"What's the matter this time, Janik?" asked she.

"May I have another ball, please, ma'am, in exchange for the cow?" said Janik.

"You may! And I hope it will do you good!" said the little old woman. "Take it home and try it."

Janik touched his cap, put the ball in his pocket and went home. He shut the door and the window, placed the ball on the table, and clapped his hands.

"Ahem," said he,

>"Ball, whenever my hands I clap,
>Remember your manners and raise your cap!"

Off the table came the ball with a bump and out bounced two men. And then, you should have heard the noise – the yells and the screams and the howls. The two men had sticks, and they beat Janik till he cried for mercy. Whack – bang – drub – drub – drub. Over the chairs he jumped, yelping like a puppy. Whack – bang – drub – drub – drub. Janik jumped over the table. He hid behind the curtains. He climbed on to the mantelpiece, but he couldn't escape. Only when he lay on the floor howling like a naughty child, did they give him one last whack and jumped back into the ball.

Janik was black and blue, but he knew what to do. When he had recovered his breath, he picked up the ball and went to see the wicked farmer.

"If you please, sir," said Janik, "I've got a new ball: it's bigger than the other. If you give me back the old one, you can have this."

"No doubt! No doubt! Janik!" said the farmer, "but I'm too old a bird to be caught. You show me what the new ball can do."

"Ahem!" cried Janik, clapping his hands,

>"Ball, whenever my hands I clap,
>Remember your manners and raise your cap!"

I needn't tell you what happened, need I? I needn't tell you how that farmer shouted.

Whack – bang – drub – drub – drub.

"Save me! Save me!" cried the farmer.

"Give me back my ball," said Janik.

Whack – bang – drub – drub – drub.

"Ow – oo," cried the farmer, "take your ball – your horrible old ball. Ow – oo! Stop! Ow! It's in the cupboard."

Janik went to the cupboard, and there, on the top shelf, was his old ball. He put it in his pocket and ran out of the farmer's house, just as the two men with the sticks jumped back into the new ball, which bounced out of the door, rolled away and was never seen again.

So Janik and Ludmila lived happily ever after, and as for Baabaa, I suppose if she's not dead, she must be still alive.

Monty Mean and Generous Jack

Anne Lidall

Once upon a time there was a man called Monty Mean. His real name was Montague Flynn, but everybody called him Monty Mean because he never gave anything away. He wouldn't help the poor and he wouldn't share anything with anybody.

He was a very rich man, and he was always buying things for himself. Some of the things he bought were no good to him, but would he give them away? Of course not. He just used to store them up in his house and gloat over them.

As the years went by he began to get rather short of space in his house. All the cupboards were full of things he never used. The bath was full of jam. The hall cupboard was full of walking sticks. He couldn't get into the pantry for all the tins and bottles he had in there. And he couldn't get into bed because it was piled high with boots and shoes.

Next door to Monty Mean lived a man called Generous Jack. It was easy to see why he was called that, because his house was almost empty. He had given everything away except a few cooking pots, a bed and a chair. He had very little money, but what he had he shared with those who had none, and he never bought any-thing for himself except what he needed to keep himself alive.

The time came when Monty Mean's house was so full that he couldn't get into any of the rooms. The staircase was stacked from top to bottom with possessions. The hall was packed to the ceiling. There was just enough space behind the front door for him to lie down in, and there he used to sleep.

He went out one afternoon to buy a few more things. It was quite dark when he got back home. He pushed his way into his house, arranged his new possessions around him, and went to sleep.

In the morning he woke up and looked round. "How I should like a nice cup of tea," he said to himself, but he couldn't get into his kitchen. "How I should like to watch my television set," he said, but he couldn't get into the living room. "How I should like a nice hot bath," he went on, but how could he have a bath in a bath full of jam?

"Never mind," he consoled himself, "I'll go out and buy myself something instead."

He tried to get to his feet, but he found that all his boxes and packages were pressing round him. He tried to open the front door, but the things he had bought the day before were holding it tightly shut. He couldn't get up and he couldn't get out.

Oh dear, what could he do? He began to cry out, "Help, help!" and fortunately Generous Jack heard his cries and came running round to see what was the matter.

"I'm stuck in here!" cried Monty Mean. "I can't open my own front door. I can't move an inch. I shall have to stay here for ever!" And he began to moan and groan.

Generous Jack thought it was time that Monty Mean was taught a lesson.

"I'll help you," he said.

"I knew you would," sighed Monty Mean.

"I'll make a bargain with you," said Generous Jack.

"Anything, anything," cried Monty Mean.

"Will you change houses with me?" asked Generous Jack. "You shall have my empty house and I will have your full house. There's a nice warm bed in my house, and a kettle and a teapot in the kitchen, all you need to make yourself comfortable."

"But what about all my beautiful things?" cried Monty Mean. "What about my boots and shoes, my walking sticks, my bath full of jam, and all the other things I have?"

"Don't worry about them," laughed Generous Jack. "I'll give them all away."

"No, no, no!" cried Monty Mean. "I can't do it, I can't!"

"Then you'll just have to stay there," said Generous Jack through the letter box. "I'll come back next week and see how you are getting on."

"No, don't go!" shouted Monty Mean as Generous Jack pretended to go away. "I'll agree to what you say. After all, I can always fill up your house with new things. I shall enjoy doing that."

So Generous Jack got a chopper and chopped down the front door and Monty Mean scrambled out. He ran round to Generous Jack's house to make a nice cup of tea, leaving Generous Jack in possession of his old house.

Time went by. Generous Jack was very happy finding things in the house to give to people who needed them. Monty Mean didn't change his ways, but went on buying things he didn't need, just to look at. He filled up Generous Jack's old house right to the front door again, and Generous Jack emptied Monty Mean's old house, except for a few cooking pots, a bed and a chair.

And can you guess what they did when that happened?

That's right. They changed houses again.

Dark Windy Night

When I was out walking
One dark windy night
I heard something behind me
One dark windy night
A footstep, a whisper
One dark windy night
A shadow before me
One dark windy night
Moonlight behind me
One dark windy night.
I shivered, I shook,
I did get a fright
When I was out walking
That dark windy night.

Anne English

"Whether the weather be fine"

Whether the weather be fine,
Or whether the weather be not,
Whether the weather be cold,
Or whether the weather be hot,
We'll weather the weather
Whatever the weather
Whether we like it or not.

Anon

Joe's House

Tessa Morris-Suzuki

"We're going to live in a house," said Joe to the other boys. "It's got five rooms and a big cellar and a bath, and there's a bit of grass at the back where we'll keep Snap, the dog. I'm going to have a room of my own."

Joe had never slept in a house before. Of course he had visited people who lived in houses, his cousins and his Mum's friends and his teacher. But always at night he came back to sleep in the trailer on the camp site, which was in the middle of an old airfield. It had been Joe's home for almost as long as he could remember. He knew every tree, every hole in the ground, every blade of grass that pushed up through the broken tarmac.

Now they were moving. They were going to live in a house. Joe felt excited, and pleased. And secretly, a little bit afraid.

Moving day was two weeks before Christmas. Uncle Jasper took them in his shiny new Range Rover. All the furniture from the trailer had to be packed in the car. There were pots and pans, tables and chairs, and Mum's best china carefully wrapped up in newspaper. Two beds were tied to the roof.

Mum sat in front with little Gary on her knee. Joe and the twins and Snap the dog went in the back, squashed up uncomfortably with bits of furniture sticking into their backs.

There had seemed to be so much furniture when they piled it into the car; but when they had taken it out and put it all in the house the rooms still looked very empty. The house was cold, and there was a funny, damp smell.

In the trailer, even on the coldest days, you only had to put on the fire and it was as warm as toast. But even when Mum had lit a coal fire the house was still cold.

Joe went upstairs and turned the bath taps on and off until Mum shouted at him to stop. Then he went down to the cellar, but it was full of spiders and the darkness frightened him.

He went outside to the bit of grass where Snap was tied up. Snap was growling. He missed his old home.

Joe looked up at the other houses in the street. Their windows stared back at him like unfriendly eyes. An old woman peered out from the house next door. She looked cross.

That night Joe woke up in the bed in his little room. He listened for the sound of the twins breathing and Gary sucking his thumb. But everything was quiet. It was strange to be in a room on his own.

Joe looked at the shadows on the ceiling. The wind rattled the window and outside Snap was whimpering. On windy nights on the camp site the trailer had rocked like a ship at sea. But the house did not rock. It just rattled and creaked a little.

Joe got out of bed. He tiptoed across the cold floor of the landing to his Mum's room and pushed open the door. His Mum was asleep, with Gary curled up in his cot beside her. Joe wanted to wake her up, but he didn't. He was too old to be afraid of the dark.

He crept back to bed.

First thing in the morning there was a knock at the door. It was the old woman Joe had seen looking out of the window. She was wearing a pink dressing-gown and her hair was in curlers.

"That blooming dog of yours," she shouted at Mum. "It kept me awake all night with its whining. This is Council property, you know. You've got no right to keep pets here."

"Oh dear," said Mum. "I didn't know. No one told us."

"You get rid of that dog at once or I'm calling the police," said the woman.

"We can't get rid of Snap. He's *mine*," wailed Joe.

"Oh, don't *you* start," cried Mum.

Then she saw the look on Joe's face and said more gently, "Don't worry, Joe. We'll get Uncle Jasper to look after him for a bit. Then we'll work something out. You'll see."

Later in the morning, when Uncle Jasper came, they explained about Snap.

"That's all right. I'll look after Snap," said Uncle Jasper. "And I'll borrow Joe for the day too. We need all the hands we can get on the site today."

As they went out of the door Joe heard sniggering further down the road. Three children stood staring at them. Then the eldest, a boy of about Joe's age, took a step forward.

"Gypsy boy, gypsy boy," he chanted, and the others giggled.

Uncle Jasper turned like a flash. He was a big strong man with hands like shovels.

"You say that again," he roared.

119

He caught hold of the boy by the collar, but the boy wriggled free and the three of them ran away, shrieking down the road with Snap at their heels.

"Little devils," muttered Uncle Jasper as he climbed into the driver's seat. Joe felt glad to be with Uncle Jasper.

They drove out of the town to a wood. Here Joe found his friends from the camp site with their Dads hard at work. Uncle Jasper and some of the other men from the site had bought two hundred Christmas trees from the owner. Now they were busy rooting them up and piling them into lorries.

Joe helped to load the trees on to a lorry. The green needles stuck to his hands. The clear, harsh smell of the trees filled the air. Although it was a cold day, Joe was soon so hot that he had to take off his jacket and roll up his sleeves. The earth on the roots of the Christmas trees made red streaks on his clothes.

Joe's best friend Charlie was there too. Joe wanted to stop and talk to him. But when he went over to the place where Charlie was working, Uncle Jasper shouted, "Come on, lad. Don't stop to chat. We haven't got all day, you know."

When the lorries were loaded up they drove them down to the camp site. Joe helped to pull off the broken and bent branches and fit the trees into little wooden blocks. His hands were sore from splinters and his back ached with bending. But it was good to be with his friends, and to be doing real work, just like a grown-up man.

"How's the house then, Joe?" asked the other boys.

But Joe just shrugged. "All right," he said.

He looked at the place where their trailer had been, but it had gone. Mum had sold it, and the new owner had already towed it away. There was only a faint mark on the tarmac to show where it had stood.

The broken branches and the roots of the Christmas trees were thrown on to two big bonfires on the edge of the site. Soon the red flames were crackling high in the air. Woodsmoke drifted on the wind.

Tired men gathered round the fires, holding out their hands to the warmth. Uncle Jasper's brother had come down from London to buy a load of trees. His big lorry was brightly painted with patterns of flowers, and his name, "Lennie Smith" picked out in gold letters on the front.

Charlie's Mum brought them hot cups of soup and sandwiches. Then Uncle Jasper, who had a good voice, began to sing. He sang a long funny song about a boxer who always lost fights. They had all heard it before, but they laughed all the same.

"Time to go home now," said Uncle Jasper.

Joe looked up. He hadn't noticed how time had passed. Joe felt sad to leave the camp site and go back to the cold, unfriendly house. He said goodbye to Snap and got silently into the car.

When Joe got back it seemed colder than ever. The twins were quarrelling, and little Gary had just tumbled down the stairs and bumped his head. Joe sat down in front of the television, but even that didn't seem to work properly in this house. The picture on the screen flickered and wobbled.

It was almost bedtime when Joe heard the sound of a car stopping in front of the house. It was Uncle Jasper again. Joe ran to the door.

"I can't stop to talk," called Uncle Jasper. "I've just brought you something."

He opened the car door and dumped a big sack on to the road.

"What is it?" asked Joe.

"A good day's pay for a good day's work," said Uncle Jasper with a smile, and he slammed the door and drove away into the darkness.

Joe opened the sack and peered into it. Inside was a Christmas tree. A Christmas tree for their new house.

Next morning, Joe put the Christmas tree in the front window. Mum gave him fifty pence to buy some glass bobbles and tinsel, and he and the twins decorated the tree.

When Joe went out into the street he saw one of the girls from down the road staring at his house.

"Is that your Christmas tree?" she asked him.

"Yes," said Joe proudly.

"Coo," said the girl. "Isn't it big!" Her eyes were wide with envy.

Joe walked up and down the road. Several other houses had Christmas trees in their windows too. Some were made of tinsel. Some were green plastic. A few had real trees, but none of them was nearly as big as Joe's.

Joe looked at the house. It was cold and it didn't have much furniture in it yet. Mum hadn't even finished making curtains. But his house had the best Christmas tree in the whole street.

"A good day's pay for a good day's work," thought Joe. And he smiled to himself.

Joseph and the Trees

Rhoda Power

The Holy Child was asleep in a manger. Mary, his mother, lay on the ground beside him, with her head pillowed against Joseph's knee, for he had promised to watch over the baby while she rested.

For a few moments Joseph, too, had closed his eyes, and was dreaming of his home in Nazareth, when the baby gave a low cry. Mary stirred in her sleep, and Joseph looked up.

The stable was dark, but a star shone through a long crack in the roof and threw a beam of light across the manger where an ox, an ass, and a horse were pulling away the last wisps of hay. Moving gently, so as not to disturb Mary, Joseph stood up. A little shivering whimper told him that the manger was bare, and that the child had now no soft hay to lie upon and no covering to keep him warm.

With an angry word Joseph drove the animals into the far corner of the stable. "Could you not have waited until morning?" he asked, striking the ox on the flank. "See what your greed has done. The child will freeze in the cold."

The sound of the blow and a long wail of distress from the baby woke Mary. She lifted herself on her elbow. "Dear Joseph," she said, "do not strike the poor beasts. The hay was theirs. If they were too hungry to lend it to us, we have no right to be angry. Give me the child, and I will wrap him in my mantle."

Still grumbling, Joseph lifted the baby from the manger and put him into Mary's arms.

But the blue mantle, which Mary had spread to dry on the wheel of an old wagon, was of no use. It was still wet with the snow which had been falling when she and Joseph had taken refuge in the stable.

Joseph looked at the shivering child, and his eyes were sad. "No one will help us," he said bitterly. "The man and his wife would not take us at the inn, and the animals will not lend the hay to warm us and the child. Everyone is against us."

"No one is against us," answered Mary, rocking the baby and looking gently at Joseph. "The innkeeper and his wife lent us their stable because we were tired and their house was so full that they could not take us in. The animals gave us their manger because there was no cradle for the child. The people and the beasts have helped us, perhaps the trees will be kind, too. Dear Joseph, tell them that we are cold and need some branches for a fire."

Then Joseph gathered his sheepskin coat around him, opened the stable door, and went out into the snow.

The ground was white, but the flakes had stopped falling and the air was very clear in the starlight. The giant trees stretched their leafless branches towards the sky, and here and there a little icicle hung like a jewel from the end of a twig. There were fig trees and olives, small stunted oaks, and a withered holly. In those days the holly had no red berries and its leaves were not evergreen but fell in the autumn, so that the branches were bare. It looked so shapeless and ugly that Joseph twitched his coat away in disgust when one of its branches caught on the wool. He turned and looked at the fig tree.

"When the sun shines, the fig has so much fruit," thought Joseph, "that it will not miss a few dead twigs. I will ask the fig."

But the fig tree was indignant. "Do you know what you're asking?" it said.

"Just a few sticks to make a fire for a child who is cold," pleaded Joseph.

"At all times of the year," answered the fig tree haughtily, "my branches lend beauty to the hillside. In the warm weather they are laden with fruit, and the children of Bethlehem rejoice in them. Even when I have no fruit, my silver bark is a joy to all who look at it. Shall this loveliness be burnt for the sake of one child, when so many enjoy it? No, find your sticks elsewhere, old man."

Distressed and disappointed, Joseph turned away. The air was growing very cold, and he was troubled. He hastened up the hill, searching to right and to left, until he came to a group of olive trees. They looked so soft and lovely in the starlight that he was sure they would help him.

"Trees," said he, "in a stable near the inn a little child is dying of cold. He has no fire. Give me, I pray you, a few pieces of your bark for fuel, that I may warm him and his mother."

"Did you hear that?" shrilled the eldest olive tree, its branches trembling with anger. "We who give oil and fruit to all the hungry children of Bethlehem are to be stripped of the bark, which keeps us warm, because a strange child is cold. Go back to your own home and get wood."

123

"Yes, go back to your own home," echoed the other olive trees; "find your fuel there, old man."

So once again Joseph passed on. He stood before the oaks. "Will you give a handful of twigs?" he asked; "there's a child in the stable, and he is crying with the cold. If I do not make him a fire, he will die."

But the oaks answered roughly, "Leave us alone. Why should we make ourselves bare and ugly for a stranger, when the children of Bethlehem love us? In the spring they decorate their houses with our leaves, and in the autumn they play without acorns and oak apples. The more twigs you burn, the fewer leaves and fruit shall we bear. Begone, and find your firewood elsewhere."

Sadly Joseph retraced his steps.

"Mary was wrong," he thought. "All the trees are against us."

Just at that moment something pulled his sheepskin coat – it was the ugly holly-tree.

"Let me help you, Joseph," it said, "no one will miss me, because I am so brown and ugly. I have no fruit for the children to eat or to play with. My leaves are so prickly that no one picks them to decorate the houses, and they die so soon that they give no beauty to the hillside. This is the only time a child has wanted something which I can give. Take me, Joseph."

So Joseph loosened the earth around the roots of the holly, and pulling the tree out of the ground, carried it back on his shoulder to the stable: he broke it in pieces and made a fire.

All night long the branches burned with a steady flame, and all night long the stable was warm and the baby slept peacefully. In the morning, when the fire had died down, clusters of scarlet embers glowed in a heap on the ground, and still the stable was warm.

"Poor little holly-tree!" said Joseph; "There is nothing left."

"Happy little holly-tree!" said Mary, "it has warmed the Christ-child. Because of this every holly-tree all the world over shall have leaves that are always green and berries as red as the embers of this fire. And when children remember the Christ-child's birthday, they will make their homes beautiful with holly."

Ever since that night the holly has been an evergreen with berries red as fire, and people bring it home at Christmas.

The Young Skier

A. William Holmes

The snow had fallen early that winter, and from the window of his room Alex could see the rounded hill slopes glistening white. Beyond them, he could pick out the gentle summit of Cairngorm, the highest mountain, as well as other peaks raising their white heads into the blue sky.

Alex wasn't sorry that the snow had come early, for now he would be able to ski! He had already oiled and polished his skis.

The night before, when he had come home from school, the fields had been green, and he had seen his father's sheep dotted on the hillsides, feeding. The clouds had been heavy and black, and he had remembered the snow warning in the morning's weather forecast.

"There's going to be a bad storm, Alex," his father had said, shaking his head anxiously.

Alex had agreed, but he didn't show his father that he would be glad if it snowed. He knew his father was anxious about the sheep, which gave them their living.

After tea the wind had got up, and in the growing dusk Alex had seen the first flurry of small, swirling snowflakes. Then the storm had got worse, and the gales had whipped the flakes into a white sheet which rapped against the windows. He had gone to bed happily, thinking of skiing.

Later in the night he had been awakened, not by the blizzard, though that was still blowing forcefully, but by shouts from the yard below his window. He had got out of bed and pulled aside the curtains. Through the still-swirling snow, he had seen the light of two storm lanterns, and realized that his father and the shepherd had been out on the hills to bring in the sheep. He had caught sight of the dark, active shapes of Wallace and Bruce, the sheep-dogs and heard the complaining "baas" of the sheep as they were herded into the pens for safety.

As he had jumped back into bed, he had heard his mother go downstairs to brew tea for his father who was just coming in.

"Did you manage to find all the sheep?" his mother had asked.

"We're one ewe short," was the reply, "we shall have to look for her in the morning."

"You don't think those sheep stealers have been again?"

"No sign of them," his father had replied, "but I did hear that the Mackintosh farm lost two last week."

The next morning the snow lay thick and piled up in great drifts. Alex was delighted, and he packed his skis, along with his school bag. He hoped that the teacher would take them out on to the slopes of the golf course to practise skiing, as he had done the year before.

Alex enjoyed sitting with his father in the cabin of the tractor, which pushed the farm snow-plough up the mile-long drive to the main road. The snow shot out on each side of them, like the white bubbling water in the wake of a great ship.

At the main road, however, Alex learned that, nearer to the town, huge drifts had blocked the road, and the snow ploughs had not yet been able to clear a way for the school bus. So after waiting a while, he trudged home.

His mother gave him hot tea and biscuits. "It's my shopping day," she said, "I really must get into town."

After lunch, his father telephoned and discovered that the road had been opened, so his mother went to do her shopping. His father was busy, so, left alone, Alex decided that he would go out and ski by himself – the first hills were so low and gentle that he could come to no harm. He got out his skis and happily stroked the smooth, polished surface of the wood. He was proud of the skis because he had made them himself. Of course, the woodwork teacher had helped him, but they were his very own.

Outside, he crossed the yard and strapped the skis on to his boots. As he did so, he looked across again to the Cairngorm mountain. When I am a little older, he thought, I shall be able to ski up there, on a real mountain and a fast slope.

Last year, his father had taken him to watch a skiing championship on those slopes. On that day he had been thrilled to see really expert skiers, some from Norway, Austria and Switzerland, glide gracefully down the long runs. Their speed was tremendous and had taken his breath away.

"I'm going to be a champion skier one day," he had told his father.

"Right, son, only you'll have to practise a lot first," his father had answered.

126

Now, crabwise as he had been taught, he began to climb the first hill. Carefully placing one ski and then the next at right angles to the slope, he climbed to the top. There, giving himself a push with his sticks, he began to slide downwards, gathering speed as he went. The cold air whizzed about his ears, and he laughed out aloud in his excitement. When he got to the bottom, he sat down in the snow. He got up carefully, and began to brush the snow from his red anorak. As he was doing this, he heard the bleat of a sheep. He knew it was a cry of distress and that the sheep couldn't be far away. He remembered hearing his father say that one had been missed in the round-up during the blizzard, and thought this must be the one! He looked carefully around, and finally found the sheep, which was lying helplessly on its back in a hole in the snow. On the hill just above it, he saw marks in the snow where the animal had tried to climb and had slipped back.

Alex knew that once a fully-grown sheep fell on its back like this, it often couldn't right itself. Immediately, he bent down and grabbed the sheep by its tail and the wool of its neck. It bleated in protest but, after a good deal of pulling and slipping about in the snow, he got it to its feet.

Then Alex noticed something. This wasn't his father's sheep! All his were marked by a blue circle on the side, and this one had a red cross on its back. He knew that the red cross was the mark used by Farmer Forbes at the farm across the valley. Whatever was this one doing here?

Still wondering about this, Alex led the sheep into the farmyard. He shut it in the enclosure with the others and then returned to the hillside.

He saw the line of disturbed snow leading to the place where he had found the sheep, so he followed the marks to the hedge which bounded the field. Still puzzled, he went through a gap in the hedge, and then stopped in surprise. There, on the track, nearly covered by drifting snow, was a small truck!

Round about the truck, he saw, in the very deep snow, men's footprints, and marks which might have been made by other sheep.

It was then that he remembered the sheep stealers, and realized what must have happened. The thieves, coming away from the Forbes farm, must have taken the wrong turning in the blizzard and then got stuck in the drift.

Quickly now, using his skis to real purpose, he hurried back to

127

the farm and telephoned Mr Forbes, who told him that he *had* lost three sheep in the night, and had seen signs of a truck on a patch of road which had become uncovered as the snow drifted about.

Alex was so excited that he could hardly wait to tell his parents about it. When they were all home again, he told them the whole story. "And I thought it was the one you couldn't find last night," he ended.

"No," said his father, "that ewe was outside the pens when I went out this morning; ours are all safe."

It wasn't long before Mr Forbes arrived with the police. They took Alex to the hillside and the thieves' abandoned truck, asking him all kinds of questions. He felt very important, and was sorry for the police, stumbling about in the snow which came over the tops of their Wellington boots, while, on his skis, he glided easily over the drifts.

At the end, the police sergeant patted him on the back. "Good work, son," he said. "Now that we've got the number of the truck, we'll find the thieves."

That night, Alex gave his skis a special polish and put them away – but only until the next day. "To be a champion, you must practise a lot," his father had said.